ECONOMIC THINKING FOR THE THEOLOGICALLY MINDED

Samuel Gregg

University Press of America,® Inc.
Lanham · New York · Oxford

Copyright © 2001 by
University Press of America,® Inc.
4720 Boston Way
Lanham, Maryland 20706
UPA Acquisitions Department (301) 459-3366

12 Hid's Copse Rd.
Cumnor Hill, Oxford OX2 9JJ

Library of Congress Cataloging-in-Publication Data

Gregg, Samuel, 1969-
Economic thinking for the theologically minded / Samuel Gregg.
p.   cm
Includes bibliographical references.
1. Economics—Religious aspects—Christianity. I. Title.

BR115.E3 G73 2001   261.8'5—dc21   2001043093 CIP

ISBN 0-7618-2096-5 (cloth : alk. paper)
ISBN 0-7618-2097-3 (pbk. : alk. paper)

∞™ The paper used in this publication meets the minimum
requirements of American National Standard for Information
Sciences—Permanence of Paper for Printed Library Materials,
ANSI Z39.48—1984

Religion and economics are contrary voices, and we can only gain by dialogue between them. Religion will always urge us to look heavenward. Economists will remind us that we are creatures set on earth. Religion reminds us of our wider commitments. Economists insist that noble motives do not always yield the best results. There is no reason why both cannot accept the integrity of the other while checking trespasses into domains not its own.

Professor Jonathan Sacks
Chief Rabbi
United Hebrew Congregations of
Great Britain and the Commonwealth

To the Greater Glory of God

CONTENTS

PREFACE

Every year, many individuals pursuing theological studies, as well as numerous Protestant, Orthodox, and Catholic seminarians undertake courses in social ethics at divinity schools, seminaries, and schools of theology across the world. Although the content of these courses varies, each class is invariably confronted with questions arising from the reality of phenomena such as poverty and unemployment, not to mention complex issues such as just-wage levels and industrial disputes. It is appropriate that seminarians study such subjects. Though it is ultimately transcendental in its inspiration and fulfillment, the Gospel of the Lord Jesus Christ has profound implications for temporal affairs. The demands of the Gospel are, of course, of a profoundly moral nature, but the Christian life is not limited to the proper ordering of personal moral life. As Germain Grisez comments, it has a social dimension, not least because social life presents us with dilemmas to which we must respond by freely acting in ways that meet the Gospel's demands.[1] The proclamation that Jesus Christ is Lord does not mean that Christ's demands can somehow be confined to one's private life. For, while the Gospel contains important directives about how we should order our personal lives, the same moral commandments have implications for how we try to order the social and political world. Thus, whatever is meant by the widely used expression "separation of church and state," it does not mean, as George Weigel observes, that Christians believe in or accept "the separation of religion from public life, or the proscription of religiously grounded argument from public life."[2]

Despite the attention given in seminaries and schools of theology to public policy issues, it is curious that few seminarians are currently exposed to one subject that is especially relevant to matters such as poverty: economics. As an intellectual discipline, economics has a potentially important role to play in the development of Christian social thought. Christian clergy, theologians, and philosophers engaged in the study of what is often described as "the social question" risk failing to grasp much of the complexity of social issues if they lack a basic understanding of the insights offered by economics. There are few Christian moral philosophers today who, in articulating their ideas about the sanctity of life from conception to natural death, have not explored science's growing insights into the development of the human person in the womb. Hence, when it comes to questions involving matters such as political economy or business, it seems reasonable to expect Christian clergy to have a general familiarity with foundational economic principles. While a life of prayer, study of Scripture, and pursuit of virtue are integral to the formation of Christians, those who wish to be of genuine assistance to the economically disadvantaged and marginalized surely need some understanding of the workings of a modern economy. Unfortunately, many theological schools and seminaries do not offer courses that provide their students with such knowledge.

It is true that most seminaries seek to alert their students to the realities of the poor and marginalized by requiring them, for example, to spend some time working with the homeless. But while these activities often bring seminarians face-to-face with the underside of modern economic life, it is rare for them to engage in a systematic and philosophical discussion of economic principles. Yet how can the morality of the act of dismissing employees be properly discerned if there is no appreciation of how the process of supply and demand affects businesses? Right thought (orthodoxy) must surely and necessarily precede right action (orthopraxis).

To make this point is not to claim that everyone working or training for ministry requires a sophisticated grasp of economics. Nor should courses in economics be given the same importance as the study of Scripture or moral theology. Indeed, we sometimes need to be reminded that the priority of Christian social ethics is not effectiveness *per se*. Stanley Hauerwas contends that, instead of "attempting to make the world more peaceable and just," the "first social ethical task of the church is to be the church."[3] This primarily means that the church should tell its story and witness to the truth about God. Hence, while Christians should care for the needy and the poor (who are not confined to the materially poor), we should do so according to the church's distinctive priorities rather than to those of the "world."

Making sense of the modern world can be a challenging and frustrating exercise. The sheer number of issues that confront us—unemployment, worker exploitation, the encroaching culture of death—sometimes seems overwhelming. Yet, for all the word's complexity, Christians cannot ignore it, not least because they have some important messages to impart to its inhabitants. Christ's final charge to us was to "go make disciples of all the nations; baptize them in the name of the Father and of the Son and of the Holy Spirit and teach them to observe all that I have commanded you!" (Mt 28:19–20).[4] This is not a directive to remain passive: We are *commanded* to be *evangelical*—to win the world for Christ. To this end, the theologian Carl Henry encourages Christians not to retreat into a ghetto, but, instead to assume responsibility to be the light of the world and the salt of the earth:

> While the Christian movement needs to challenge the dogma that political means will solve all the problems of mankind, it may not neglect to use these means for the achieving of proper and legitimate objectives. The Church must expound the revealed will of God for the political order no less than for the other spheres of life, for all are answerable and subject to divine judgment.[5]

If, then, Christians are to speak in the public square, it is appropriate for them to be exposed to some of the fundamental premises of economics. It is for this reason that this brief primer on economics was composed. While this text does not attempt to provide detailed insights into the technical aspects of economic theory, it does seek to introduce readers to basic economic principles. Although the Lord's commandment to love and help the poor is ultimately an encounter between individuals, Christians cannot afford to neglect the insights that economists can offer into these problems. Indeed, one hopes that one day there will be a more sophisticated integration of basic economic principles into the social justice component that is a common feature of contemporary seminary curriculum.

The first part of this book provides an introduction to what economist Paul Heyne has called the "economic way of thinking."[6] This involves explaining some of the critical concepts and foundational assumptions employed in economics. To communicate these ideas effectively to those engaged in theological education, this book avoids unnecessary technical terminology. These concepts and assumptions are then subject to analysis from the standpoint of Christian ethics, with emphasis placed upon illustrating the often-unsuspected degree of agreement between economics and Christian belief about the nature of the human person.

The second part consists of a collection of selections from classic economic texts, representing a range of authors from a variety of schools of thought. These selections have been arranged around ten key concepts, each of which attempts to deepen understanding of various ideas presented in the first part of the book. A short introduction accompanies each selection, explaining its context and primary significance.

As readers make their way through both parts, however, they should remain conscious of the following caveat: Economics provides us with only a limited insight into the nature of the human condition. Those who believe that it can explain everything about the human person and society have fallen into the trap of absolutizing these insights. This common error of mistaking *a* truth for the *whole* truth on the part of some professional economists should not, however, deter Christians from seeking to understand what the discipline of economics can tell us about the world. Christians have no reason to be afraid of truth because, ultimately, we believe that all truth is grounded in the One who described himself as "*the* Way, *the* Truth and *the* Life" (Jn 14:6). It is ultimately from this standpoint that this book attempts to provide an introduction to economics for the theologically minded, not least because economics—unlike so many other contemporary humanistic disciplines—unashamedly affirms that there is truth for man to discover.

Notes

1. See Germain Grisez, *The Way of the Lord Jesus*, vol. 2, *Living a Christian Life* (Quincy, Ill.: Franciscan Press, 1993), 261–62.

2. George Weigel, "Towards the Third Millennium" (speech delivered at the Becket Fund for Religious Liberty's Conference on Secularism and Religious Liberty, Rome, 7 December 1995), 6. See also Richard John Neuhaus, *The Naked Public Square: Religion and Democracy in America* (Grand Rapids, Mich.: Eerdmans Publishing Company, 1984).

3. Stanley Hauerwas, *The Peaceable Kingdom* (Notre Dame: University of Notre Dame Press, 1983), 99.

4. *Jerusalem Bible* (London: Darton, Longman & Todd, 1966).

5. Carl Henry, *Aspects of Christian Social Ethics* (Grand Rapids, Mich.: Eerdmans Publishing Company, 1964), 76.

6. See Paul Heyne, *The Economic Way of Thinking*, 8th ed. (Englewood, N.J.: Prentice Hall, 1997).

ACKNOWLEDGMENTS

I thank the Calvin K. Kazanjian Economics Foundation for its generous support of this book, and Stephen Grabill for his editorial efforts, especially in regard to Part II. I also wish to thank Professor Ian Harper of the University of Melbourne for discussions of this book's subject matter over a number of years. I can think of few others who manage to combine their commitment to economics and the economics profession with an even firmer commitment to the Lord Jesus Christ.

Part I

CHAPTER 1

CHRISTIAN SOCIAL ETHICS

The message of Jesus Christ is addressed to each and every human person. At some stage of our lives, we as individuals have to decide whether we do believe that Jesus of Nazareth is indeed "the Christ, the Son of the Living God" (Mt 16:16), our Redeemer, and the Lord of history. Our decision to believe or not to believe has profound implications for the way that we live our individual lives, for if we love God, then we *obey* his commandments (1 Jn 5:3).

At the best of times, this will always be difficult, but in the modern world, it is surely even harder. The temptation to view God's commandments as "helpful suggestions," or "ideals" (which, because they are ideals, we should not be too disappointed at not fulfilling) is great. More than one contemporary theologian has strayed down the path of trying to justify an approach to the moral life that eschews Christianity's evocation of moral absolutes from the very beginning.[1] In an age dominated by the prevalence of crude and sophisticated versions of relativism throughout much of the academy and popular culture, the proposition that there is more to the good life than simply being "tolerant" or "not hurtful" is difficult to explain to much of the modern world.

Central, of course, to the Christian moral message is the Lord's commandment to love our neighbors as ourselves. This underscores the social dimension of living a Christian life. Such a way of life embraces the idea of relationship. This relationship is with God the Father, God the Son, and God the Holy Spirit. The Lord's command to love other human beings nonetheless makes it clear that the Christian immersion into relationship directs one toward concern for family, friends, the immediate

3

Christian community, and humanity as a whole. Christians are thus obliged to become aware of the scope and needs of the wider human family.

Human Dignity and the Quest for Justice

The call to relationship with others reflects the church's awareness of the integral equality of dignity enjoyed by every human being. Gentile or Jew, servant or free, woman or man—Christianity has always held that all humans are made in the Image of God. It is nonetheless true that, perhaps to a greater extent than at any other time, the twentieth century witnessed an immense growth in awareness of our dignity as persons. This may be due to the terrible violation of this dignity in the systematic policies of humiliation and annihilation adopted by totalitarian regimes of the Left and the Right. Though there are good reasons to be concerned about the extent to which the language of human rights is presently employed to bolster a range of policies that undermine human dignity, the unprecedented philosophical and juridical recognition of what are commonly called *human rights* reflects widespread recognition that each individual enjoys the same dignity as a human person—a dignity that is not dependent on variables such as economic status, race, or religion.

If we recognize that each person enjoys the same dignity, it follows that Christians believe that everyone is owed certain protections and enjoys certain entitlements. These are considered to be the subject matter of justice. In the natural-law tradition—founded by Aristotle and absorbed into the Christian tradition by the apostle Paul, the medieval scholastics, as well as Protestants such as Samuel von Pufendorf and Hugo Grotius—justice is understood to involve giving people their due or what is rightly theirs. This view of justice meshes with the scriptural understanding of justice derived from the relational character of Christianity—namely, the need to be in right relationship with others and with God.

Both concepts of justice force us to examine the character of the social order in which we live—how we order all our relationships and give all others their due, not just those closest to us. For obvious reasons, our relationships and obligations to those in close proximity to us are much easier to grasp and fulfill than our responsibilities to unknown individuals in foreign lands. Yet Christianity insists that our responsibilities of justice do not stop at the borders of our families or nations.

If, however, we are to act justly toward our neighbor—in short, to act in solidarity with our neighbor—we must freely choose to do so. For if solidarity is a virtue, then it must be consciously practiced and chosen; it cannot be coerced. While societies may, in the short term, be able to enforce a social order that meets the formal demands of strict justice and solidarity, such an order would be morally empty; it would also constitute an affront to human dignity insofar as it would deny the crucial elements of individual right reasoning and free choice that are central to the good life.

As Christians, we also know that our solidarity with all humanity involves special attention to the poor and disadvantaged. Christ could hardly have been more explicit about this. In our contemporary context, the people of the developing world, for example, merit particular attention, as do the disabled, the elderly, and the most defenseless persons: unborn children.

Though our obligation as Christians to assist the poor and marginalized is not in doubt, we need to remember that the issue of *how* we help the poor is more complex. In the first place, helping the disadvantaged means precisely that: assisting the poor rather than usurping their free will and reason. While it is possible to give people everything they need and/or desire, this does not help them to *self*-realize the basic moral goods or virtues that reflect our consistent free choice for the good. Endowed with intellect and free will, each person is responsible for his or her self-fulfillment. Naturally, each person may be helped—or hindered—in fulfilling this objective by those around him or her; but whatever the external influences, each person is ultimately responsible for his or her own acquisition of spiritual, moral, and material goods. Only by freely choosing can the human person interiorize such goods and grow toward the ultimate happiness that is oneness with God, the first Truth and highest Good.

This need to allow people to self-realize moral and spiritual goods places certain restrictions on our ability to act justly toward others. If, on the one hand, we do not allow them room to make free choices for good or evil, then we effectively stifle this aspect of human development. On the other hand, if we do not help them to acquire the level of material well-being that most people require before they can even begin to think about higher things, then their capacity to self-actualize the goods that prefigure our transcendent destiny becomes circumscribed.

Christians thus understand that the stakes are indeed high when we think about how best to arrange the social, economic, and political order so that the conditions that allow all to fulfill themselves are optimized. Competing duties and rights need to be reconciled; attention needs to be paid to the importance of self-actualizing the virtues; and help must not be configured so as to facilitate dependency. Envisaging the realization of a social order that manages to meet all of these criteria is perhaps an exercise in utopianism. As Christians, we know that the kingdom of God is not of this world. What can be said, however, is that Christianity's commitment to justice and its affirmation of the inherent dignity of all human persons implies, at a minimum, a willingness to create a social order in which people are free to participate in all aspects of social life— including its economic dimension.

Justice in the Economic Sphere

Where, one may ask, does the material world fit into this schema? How do we order economic life so that it contributes to the conditions that allow all people to undertake the great task of transforming themselves from the "person-I-am" to the "person-I-ought-to-be"?

In the first instance, it would seem that justice in the area of material goods involves increasing opportunity for creative participation in the productive sector by expanding the possibilities for employment, wealth creation, and property ownership. These are important not simply because they provide more space for people to acquire material goods but also because the very acts associated with the emergence, growth, and maintenance of these phenomena allow people to cultivate virtues such as prudence, courage, and industriousness. Hence, while justice does not necessarily entail *giving* people unmerited employment or unearned wealth, it certainly does involve allowing them to *earn* such things or create such wealth.

There is, however, another dimension to justice in the economic sphere. This involves the Christian acknowledgement of responsibility to others. Christianity has, for example, always placed its stress on the inviolability of private property within the context of the obligations of stewardship as well as what is often referred to as the *universal destination of material goods* (or what some call the *common use principle*). This reflects the Gospel truth that the earth is be used by and on behalf of all people. This does not mean that in the beginning all human persons jointly owned the material earth, with each having an equal share. Rather, it means that nothing in subhuman creation ever comes with a label saying: "This good is meant for this person but not that one, this group but not that group." It simply means that in the beginning as well as now, God provides material goods for the use of all. The question of *how* the earth's resources are to be used for the benefit of all is basically left to people to work out with the guidance of Scripture and right reason.[2] The Decalogue provides us with such guidance in its prohibition against stealing. "Thou shalt not steal" (Ex 20:2–17; Dt 5:6–21; Mt 19:18) implicitly invests private property arrangements with special significance, not least because right reason tells us that they are the best means of realizing the principle of common use.[3]

Then there is the fact that Christians are called upon to form unique bonds of solidarity with the poor, the destitute, and the lonely, and to help those who cannot help themselves. Christians do not interpret in narrow or materialistic terms the Lord's commandment to love the poor. Moral and spiritual poverty are, in many senses, more crippling than a dearth of material goods. Nonetheless, throughout the centuries, Christians have sought to give effect to the Lord's exhortations to help the materially poor by engaging in a variety of charitable activities. Pagans in the Roman world (where life was notoriously cheapened) were astounded not only by the reverence for life displayed by Jews and Christians but also the care offered by Jewish and Christian communities to the materially underprivileged. We know, of course, that the effects of sin will not be fully reversed prior to the Lord's final coming. Nevertheless, Christ calls upon his people to minister to those who suffer any form of undue deprivation *now*.

Yet, if we are to understand poverty properly, it is surely true that, among other things, a grasp of economics must first be acquired. Not all poverty proceeds directly from economic deprivation, but we will fail to comprehend completely the causes of poverty and its persistence without such an understanding. The Christian who wishes to comment and act responsibly—rather than in an emotivist manner—when dealing with such issues surely requires some knowledge of essential economic theory.

For centuries, many Christian clergy and laypeople have grappled intellectually with the problem of how to build a genuinely humane economic system grounded in a correct understanding of the human person. In the course of such reflection, many have wandered into error. This was true of some liberation theologians in the 1970s and 1980s who did not take full account of the profoundly materialist anthropology of the human person that underlies Marxist thought, or who simply accepted Marxism's dialectical materialist methodology. There have, however, been many Christians who, without presuming that they have discovered the whole truth about economic life or claiming to speak for the church, have been willing to offer their own prudential judgments about the economic dimension of human life based upon a genuinely Christian anthropology of man.

Ministry to the marginalized is not, of course, only about material possessions; it is also about forging communion between persons. Christians are obliged to give more than money to provide for people's needs. The Lord demands that we give ourselves—to love, care for, and become involved in the lives of those we serve. Although this is seldom easy, it becomes even more arduous if we lack a basic understanding of economics, given the extent to which questions surrounding the production and exchange of material goods dominate discussions of matters ranging from globalization to just wages.

Economics as an intellectual discipline is not, however, viewed entirely favorably within the Christian community. As one economist and Christian remarks, economics is "often assumed to be little more than materialist propaganda by some Christians."[4] It follows that there is a need to familiarize many Christians with the nature and limits of economics as an intellectual discipline, not least because such an undertaking will help us to identify more readily the types of questions that economics can help us to answer—and those it cannot.

Notes

1. For a detailed discussion of this problem, see John Finnis, *Moral Absolutes: Tradition, Revision, and Truth* (Washington, D.C.: Catholic University of America Press, 1990), 84–105; and Samuel Gregg, *Morality, Law, and Public Policy* (Sydney, Australia: Saint Thomas More Society, 2001): 81–96.

2. The respective treatments of this question by Saint Thomas Aquinas and Vatican II are especially instructive. See Saint Thomas Aquinas, *Summa Theologiae* (London: Blackfriars, 1975): II-II, q. 66, a. 2; and Second Vatican Council, Pastoral Constitution on the Church in the Modern World (*Gaudium et Spes*), 7 December 1965, no. 69, in *Vatican Council II: The Conciliar and Post-Conciliar Documents*, vol. 1, rev. ed., ed. A. Flannery, O.P. (Leominster, U.K.: Fowler Wright Books Ltd., 1988).

3. For an extended discussion of this point, see Grisez, *Living a Christian Life*, 789–91.

4. Samuel Gregg and Ian Harper, *Economics and Ethics: The Dispute and the Dialogue* (Sydney, Australia: The Centre for Independent Studies, 1999), 3.

CHAPTER 2

MAKING SENSE OF ECONOMICS

Thomas Carlyle, a nineteenth-century political philosopher, once described economics as the "dismal science" on account of the (yet to be proven) dire consequences of unchecked population growth predicted by the Reverend Thomas Malthus, who, along with Adam Smith and David Ricardo, is one of the intellectual founders of modern economics. On another occasion, Carlyle accused economists of embracing a "pig philosophy." He appears to have been no admirer of economists or economics.

We should not be surprised, therefore, to find on the one hand that some Christians follow Carlyle in viewing economics with suspicion, even rejecting outright the claim that people can be studied with the same detachment as inanimate objects. On the other hand, there are many Christian thinkers (or economists who also happen to be confessing Christians) who are happy to make use of social science research methods without necessarily accepting all the philosophical premises that underlie them.

Broadly speaking, economics may be described as the study of the production, distribution, and consumption of scarce goods and services. Economists study how people satisfy the basic requirements for daily living. To put it differently, economics is the study of how free persons choose to cooperate through voluntary exchanges to satisfy their own and others' needs in light of the reality of limited resources.

But what research methods and what presumptions underlie the manner in which economics stuies this question? Those intersted in unraveling this mystery need to understand a crucial distinction: the difference between positive and normative economics.

9

Positive Economics

In the history of Western thought, the emergence of modern economics as an autonomous intellectual discipline is relatively recent. In the Aristotelian and Scholastic traditions, economics and politics were studied as part of a broader inquiry into ethics under the title of *philosophia moralis*.[1] Even in the European universities of the 1700s, economics was still taught as part of moral philosophy.[2]

Economics gradually emerged as an autonomous science, not least because, as the economist and Anglican thinker, Lord Griffiths, points out, the Enlightenment encouraged people to think about economics as well as many other subjects in a more abstract, even amoral (as distinct from immoral), manner.[3] Modern economic theory subsequently stresses that the judgments made by individuals within economic processes involve subjective valuation. As Peter Boettke notes, "It is precisely the radical subjectivism of economics that assures us that the discipline has any way to approximate 'objective knowledge.'"[4] Economics does not, for example, attempt to determine whether profits are deserved. Rather, it seeks to tell us *how* profit has been realized, and it would be severely distracted from undertaking this task in a reasonably objective manner if the question of deservedness were the centerpiece of the analysis.

In his book on post-Enlightenment economics, Lionel Robbins defines economics as "the science which studies human behavior as a relationship between ends and scarce means that have alternative uses."[5] In this sense, the primary task of economics is to determine the objective effects of different choices about how scarce goods may be used. While Ludwig von Mises's understanding of economics is similar, he prefers to speak of it as the study of human action so as to accent the central role played by free choice and acts in economics. To Mises's mind, economics

> is a theoretical "science." ... It is not its task to tell people what ends they should aim at. It is a "science" of the means to be applied for the attainment of ends chosen, not, to be sure, a "science" of the choosing of the ends.... Science never tells a man how he should act; it merely shows how a man must act if he wants to attain definite ends.[6]

Both Mises's and Robbins's definitions indicate that economics is a *positive* discipline *insofar* as it involves the study of cause-effect relationships that, if they can be demonstrated as empirically true, may be regarded as having a high degree of empirical validity. Positive economics is especially concerned with discerning changes in activity—

notably those that represent responses to alterations in economic variables and policy. What, for example, are the likely effects of tax cuts targeted at certain income segments of the population upon wealth creation and distribution? Positive economics does not, consequently, involve ethical judgments concerning these relationships; it does not ask whether the object of such decisions is good or evil.

Normative Economics

The results of the study of positive economics do, however, contribute to the formulation of economic policy. Economic policy—what some call *normative economics* or *political economy*—articulates, according to Carl Menger, "the basic principles for the suitable advancement (appropriate to conditions) of 'national economy' on the part of the public authorities."[7]

For our purposes, the most important word in Menger's statement is *suitable*. What, indeed, is suitable? In answering this question, one cannot but enter the world of philosophy, politics, and ethics. For a variety of reasons, including moral ones, some will ascribe more value to the end of freedom than that of equality, and vice versa. To this extent, the formulation of economic policy—understood as the selection of economic goals and the means of implementing them—is a normative activity. It is, therefore, a legitimate field for ethical inquiry. One may even argue that when an economist goes beyond simply pointing out the objective effects of an economic choice and renders an opinion that involves moral and/or political judgments about the means, object, and side effects of a potential or actual economic policy, he becomes less of an economist and more a public policy adviser.

A "Value-Free" Discipline?

One should, however, be aware that neither normative nor positive economics is a hard "science" in the sense that chemistry and physics purport to be "value-free" disciplines. This may be illustrated by outlining the different statements that an economist can make about taxes on cigarettes:

- *If the government increases the tax on cigarettes, people will generally smoke less.* This is a positive statement reached by logical deductions based upon certain assumptions about how people behave.

- *If the government wants to reduce the amount smoked, it should increase cigarette taxes.* This is a prescriptive statement. It does not tell us that the government should reduce smoking. Rather, it describes what a government could do if it wished to do so.
- *The government should increase the tax on cigarettes.* This is a normative statement because it is based upon the judgment that the situation after the tax increase will be generally better than the current situation.

Initially, this division seems to confirm that the difference between positive and normative economic statements lies in the judgment underscoring the latter. But on closer examination, one becomes aware that the positive statement outlined above is not as neutral as one might suppose. For what are the *assumptions* about human behavior that underlie the logical deductions on which this statement is based? One is that people generally prefer more to less: in other words, that people are utility maximizers. In itself, this would seem to be an objectively verifiable conclusion.

But another assumption is the anthropological model of *homo economicus*: the human person as the ultimate pleasure calculator. While few economists actually suggest that this model captures the complexity of human beings, it is not a neutral model. The moral-philosophical viewpoint most akin to it is essentially a crude form of utilitarianism (i.e., nothing is intrinsically good or evil). Instead, that which is "good" is what provides most people with pleasure, satisfaction, and utility, and each person's idea of what is pleasurable is purely a matter of subjective preference. Not all the assumptions, underlying positive economics, then, are philosophically neutral. This is not to say that economics is reducible to ethics. It only means, as Ricardo Crespo states, "that economics is not a value-free science."[8]

It seems, then, that economics is very much a humanistic discipline rather than a physical science. Nevertheless, the preceding summary suggests that the is-ought/positive-normative differentiation still serves as a useful dichotomy for those attempting to understand the nature of economics as a field of intellectual inquiry. Not only does the distinction enable economists to highlight the more empirical aspects of their work, but it is also a way to differentiate between economics as the study of objective facts (e.g., the fact that there *is* a relationship between supply and demand) and economics as the exposition of public policies based on both those objective facts as well as the decision to pursue selected political, social, and moral goals.

Foundational Assumptions

Although the distinction between normative and positive economics is important, it also indicates that economics as an intellectual discipline is based on certain assumptions. As noted, one of the most important of these is the anthropological model of *homo economicus*.

Homo Economicus

To make it quite clear that economics professes knowledge of humanity in only one of many dimensions, economists have invented an artificial human being. This creature, *homo economicus*, exists only as a fiction in the minds of economists, but, as with psychologists and their rats, economists hope that the study of *homo economicus* under laboratory conditions will teach them something of the ways of *homo sapiens* in the real world.

Homo economicus is the ultimate pleasure calculator. Utterly without spiritual dimension by design, this creature seeks only to maximize personal satisfaction from the consumption of goods and services. Though *homo economicus* can evince altruistic behavior, it will do so only as a means of self-satisfaction and never from any higher motive. The actions of this creature are focused on the calculation of costs and benefits from a narrowly self-interested standpoint. The same creature will evade rules if he can, and will tend to keep them only if he believes that it is in his material self-interest to do so. In short, *homo economicus* is somewhat of a sociopath.

This concept of human motivation is deliberately artificial and is intended to apply only in the narrowly economic sphere of human endeavor. Other disciplines, such as sociology, begin with an entirely different concept of human motivation. Economists aim to investigate the predictions that emerge from the close study of *homo economicus*. They ask: If we assume that people behave in economic matters as if *homo economicus* were real, how far would we be from predicting what is observed in the world? Unless—and until—the predictions of economics are consistently rejected by the data, there is no good, empirical reason to abandon what is an intentionally one-dimensional and craven view of human nature.

Having introduced our model of the rational economic human being, we can proceed directly to define *economic rationality* as a description of the behavior of *homo economicus*, faced with particular circumstances and operating under a set of principles that allow it to achieve maximum satisfaction, given the limited resources at its disposal. It follows that, when a policy is described as economically rational, the implication is that *real* people are assumed to behave in the same manner as *homo economicus* in similar circumstances and to derive satisfaction from the same sources and to the same extent as *homo economicus* does.

Reflection on *homo economicus* illustrates the limitations of economic rationality. *Homo economicus* will always be an imperfect guide to the behavior of people in the real world; the same is true of psychologists' experiments with rats. Whether such experiments tell us anything useful at all depends on how closely the idealized conditions of the laboratory conform to the more complex circumstances of reality.

Moreover, while the description of economic methodology given here conveys the impression of objectivity, an element of subjectivity cannot, in practice, be avoided. The types of questions to which economists devote their attention reflect their subjective views as to what is important for improving the material condition of humanity. *Homo economicus* will be pressed into service more vigorously in pursuing those questions that economists deem worthy of investigation, and this choice will, in turn, reflect aspects of their individual *Weltanschauung*. In this regard, however, economists are no more guilty of parading a false objectivity than are "pure" scientists, including physicists and biologists. The fact/value distinction can be sustained, but only up to a point, in any human intellectual pursuit.

Self-Interest

The pursuit of self-interest is placed at the heart of *homo economicus*'s calculations about what is the most optimal course of action. Why people choose to act in certain ways is a topic that has taxed the imagination of the most insightful philosophers, theologians, artists, and scientists. Not surprisingly, they have arrived at a range of conclusions, many of which are quite incompatible. Economists, however, make the assumption that people generally act in an instrumentally *rational* manner and that this rationality is decisively shaped by their *self-interest*. By "self-interest," they generally mean each individual's self-determined objectives, desires, and needs.

With its focus upon the human person as a self-interested rational actor, there is little question that economics provides us with insights into the nature of human activity. It is reasonable to suggest, for example, that the entrepreneur acts in certain ways in order to maximize his profit. To produce profit, entrepreneurs seek to secure labor at competitive wages that enhance anticipated productivity. Up to this point, it could be said that the self-interest of the entrepreneur is essentially egotistical.

But why, one may ask, does the entrepreneur desire to make a profit? Small-business owners may wish to do so to provide financial support to those they love. To do so, they require skilled labor and, subsequently, they hire people with such skills. Likewise, talented employees seek to sell their skills in order to support their own families.

The resulting labor arrangement—driven, in part, by both the owner's and the worker's self-interests—is thus more or less mutually beneficial to owners and employees. In the case of both employee and owner, egoistic and altruistic aspects are difficult to separate in a concrete sense. No employer or employee can afford to be completely altruistic. Yet, in following their "egoistic" motivation, they indirectly serve others. This insight is at the core of Adam Smith's famous observation concerning how the pursuit of self-interest acts as an invisible hand, bringing a type of order to the economic realm.[9]

We thus see that the issue of self-interest is more complex than one might initially suppose. Self-interest need not necessarily be equated with *selfishness*. Here Christians may have something to learn from Jewish and Muslim traditions, neither of which tends to cast quite the negative light upon the term *self-interest* as do some Christians. In these traditions, Michael Novak reminds us, self-interest is understood as a commonsense duty to oneself.[10] In this context, the Christian commandment to "Love thy neighbor as *oneself*" assumes new meaning. A fundamental and proper love of self is no cause for moral unease. Indeed, the person who does not love himself in a reasonable manner is not especially capable of loving others who are also made in God's image.

In any event, it is important to note that economists assume self-interested rational behavior when making predictions about questions such as labor costs or inflation rates. If it is reasonable to assume that all people seek to maximize their self-interest, then other assumptions can be made about economic activity.

The Fact of Scarcity

Human beings possess limited means to actualize their self-interest. From the beginning of time, humanity has been confronted with the reality of *scarcity*. Consciousness of this state of affairs is built into the heart of economics. Humans do not find that nature automatically provides us with the things that we desire or need. Work is required to harness this potential. Hence, everything that is produced by humans costs us some of our time and labor. A price is therefore always attached to each person's fulfillment of his or her self-interest.

Given that goods—and the things that we use to produce goods—are limited in supply, humans discover that they must make choices. Some things must be given up so that we can enjoy the benefits of other things. The need to choose implies the need to sacrifice. The very act of choice implies that, while one thing is chosen, another is left behind. Economists are accused, as was the prophet Jeremiah, of harping endlessly on the costs of people's actions, but they do neither more nor less than point to the self-evident fact of scarcity. The choice of option A implies the rejection of option B, and sometimes options D and E as well. It is not possible to choose everything.

While the truth of scarcity and the constraints that it imposes on our choices may seem obvious to some, many people fail to acknowledge this fundamental reality. But recognizing the inherent cost of every human decision should not carry a negative connotation. Understanding the price of something, whether it be in time, labor, or money, assists everyone in distinguishing needs from desires, thereby causing us to give some consideration to what our priorities should be. It encourages us to be wise in our choices and thus, indirectly, encourages us to actualize the first of the cardinal virtues: prudence.

The Importance of Incentives

If one accepts that the fact of scarcity and associated costs will influence human choices and actions, then it seems reasonable to posit that individual behavior is influenced by *incentives*. Economists routinely hold that incentives matter. If the benefits derived from a choice are greater than the other alternatives, then people will be more likely to choose it. Conversely, if the personal costs for an option increase, then people will be less inclined to choose it.

Few would question that incentives affect behavior in virtually every area of our lives. When it comes to the purchase of goods, prices effectively function as an incentive. People tend to search for the lowest price for a particular good or service. At the same time, we also take into account other incentives, such as the quality of the good or service. Careful observation of economic history tells us that when the price of a good increases, consumers will tend to buy less of it. Sellers, on the other hand, will supply more of that same good, as the price increase has made its production more profitable. When economists speak of *supply and demand*, this is what they generally have in mind. Incentives are critical to understanding how this "law" operates.

Mutually Beneficial Exchange

The fact of scarcity also illustrates the validity of another working assumption of economists: that people need to engage in exchanges to satisfy their desires and needs. The scarcity of immediately usable goods and services means that people face constant choices concerning their survival. These choices involve deciding upon the most effective ways of allocating resources for food, shelter, and other basic human needs.

We know, however, that natural resources and usable goods are not allocated equally. Some people enjoy more of these usable goods than others, either because of their proximity to resources or through their creativity and labor. This situation is further complicated by the fact that people are naturally unequal in their abilities and talents, but no person is in a position to say that he can do without some form of exchange; it is required for survival. Since self-sufficiency is nearly impossible to attain, most people need to enter a network of exchange to survive, and, once their needs have been met, to flourish.

Economists view the process of exchange as the best way of actualizing the material well-being of a majority of people. When an economic exchange takes place, economists hold that each person has traded something that he or she subjectively regards as having a lower value for something that has a higher value for them, given their circumstances, needs, and desires. One person may have bread, while the other has fruit. By exchanging some of their goods, each believes himself to be subjectively more prosperous than he was before the trade; otherwise, it would not have occurred.

When all participants in an economy are free to engage in exchange, a network of human interaction emerges. Economists commonly describe this as a *market*. This network of acts of exchange constantly changes and develops, primarily because what people subjectively value is constantly changing, as are the availability and type of resources that are created as a result of human ingenuity. To facilitate these acts of exchange, *money* is eventually introduced as a standard medium of exchange.

Limits and Insights

The foundational assumptions of economics that are outlined above do not even begin to encapsulate the sheer complexity of what occurs in the production, distribution, and exchange of material goods. Nevertheless, they are working assumptions commonly employed by economists in pursuing their study of this area. Naturally, there are questions that can be asked about the limits of these assumptions. In the case of *homo economicus*, for example, Christians are surely right to question those economists who actually take the step of presuming that *homo economicus* captures the entirety of human nature. This is what Novak describes as the vice of making an intellectual discipline "into an ideology . . . a denial of the legitimacy of other methods of inquiry."[11]

Despite these limitations, economics does provide us with certain insights into the truth. Does anyone seriously deny that there is a relationship between supply and demand? It would be imprudent for Christians to do this. Religious leaders, however, do have serious things to say about what happens in the countless number of freely chosen actions that constitute the market. Ethics is one field of inquiry in which the church can claim some expertise. What occurs in the market is no more exempt from the demands of truth than any other act that involves a free choice between good and evil. Yet, when we turn to the relationship between economics and the moral life, we discover that it is a more complicated phenomenon than we might initially suppose.

Notes

1. See J. E. Alvey, "A Short History of Economics As a Moral Science," *Journal of Markets and Morality* 2, 1 (Spring 1999): 55.

2. See E. R. Canterbery, *The Literate Economist* (New York: Harper Collins, 1995), 42.

3. Brian Griffiths, *The Creation of Wealth* (London: Hodder and Stoughton, 1984), 107–8.

4. Peter Boettke, "Is Economics a Moral Science? A Response to Ricardo Crespo," *Journal of Markets and Morality* 1, 2 (Fall 1998): 214.

5. Lionel Robbins, *An Essay on the Nature and Significance of Economic Science* (London: Macmillan, 1952), 16.

6. Ludwig von Mises, *Human Action: A Treatise on Economics*, 3d ed. (Chicago: Henry Regnery, 1966), 10.

7. Carl Menger, *Problems of Economics and Sociology* (Urbana, Ill.: University of Illinois Press, 1963), 211.

8. Ricardo Crespo, "Is Economics a Moral Science?" *Journal of Markets and Morality* 1, 2 (Fall 1998): 201.

9. See Adam Smith, *An Inquiry into the Nature and Causes of the Wealth of Nations*, vol. 1, ed. R. H. Campbell and W. B. Todd (Indianapolis: Liberty Classics, 1981), IV.ii.9.

10. See Michael Novak, *Catholic Social Thought and Liberal Institutions: Freedom with Justice*, 2d ed. (Oxford: Transaction Publishers, 1989), 8.

11. Novak, *Catholic Social Thought*, 7.

CHAPTER 3

ETHICS AND ECONOMICS

Our unique capacities of reason and free will allow us as human beings to embrace what no other mortal creature can: the moral life. The call to do good and avoid evil is integral to the Christian message. The Christian faith is simply incomprehensible for those who cannot grasp that our past acts and omissions really affect our present and future relationship with God. From its earliest beginnings, Christianity was called *the way*. It is an expression found seven times in the Acts of the Apostles. The apostle Paul confesses, for example, that "I persecuted this way" (Ac 22:4). This meant that Christianity was seen as a way of living. The new convictions that it brought had a directly practical content—faith, in other words, included morality. It was by living this way that faith was made visible as something new. A Christianity that no longer proclaimed a common way of right living but limited itself to proclaiming inspiring ideals or narrowing moral questions to issues of tolerance, would no longer be the Christianity of Jesus Christ.

The obligations of Christians to live in truth do not somehow cease when their thought and actions embrace the economic realm. The question thus arises: How compatible is economics as an intellectual discipline with orthodox Christian teaching about the good life? Many Christians will already recognize that there are some distinct differences, even incompatibilities between the two. Yet, close attention to some of the assumptions of economics indicates that Christian morality has more in common with the "economic way of thinking" than one might initially expect.

Is There a Specifically Christian Ethics?

Any discussion of ethics and economics must involve clarifying the character of ethics. By its very nature, ethics is a *normative* intellectual exercise. As an intellectual discipline, it is concerned with the study of voluntary human conduct; that is, all actions and omissions that people understand and will in relation to an object that they have in view. Human actions are, of course, the subject of other disciplines such as psychology and economics. But the primary interest in these fields is not what people *ought* to do but *how* and *why* they act. By contrast, the study of ethics involves knowing more than what people do. *It means asking which acts are appropriate in light of the truth about good and evil and which are not.* Broadly speaking, this involves discerning the object of an act and the intention underlying that act, as well as considering the side effects of the act and the circumstances surrounding it. The rational ordering of a freely willed human act to the good constitutes morality, but if the object of an act chosen by the will is not in harmony with the truth about the good, then it is an evil act.

Ethics may thus be defined in intellectual terms as the philosophical study of voluntary human action with the purpose of determining what activities are good, right, and to be done (or bad, wrong, and not to be done), so that people may live in truth. For, while people may know some moral principles, they will not always know what should be done in a given situation. The formal study of ethics thus seeks to help people not only by establishing what these basic moral principles are (e.g., the principle that people should receive what is due to them) but by applying them to a variety of hypothetical and actual situations. How, for example, are people to be given what they are owed in light of the reality of limited resources and the subsequent need to create more? For this reason, ethics should not be understood as consisting of a precise list of actions to be done and actions to be shunned but, rather, as an activity by which human beings reason about how they should live. This being the case, ethics is surely more than "just another discipline." It is an unavoidable and essential activity in which all people engage each time they perform a freely willed act—an activity that is intimately related to their vision of the meaning of life.

Given that, in purely intellectual terms, ethics is a philosophical exercise, some argue that there is, strictly speaking, no such thing as "Christian ethics." Others suggest that Christianity is simply one "voice" of moral discourse among many, when it comes to discussion of ethical issues.

In a very limited sense, this latter statement is true inasmuch as there are many secular and religious movements that contribute to debates about the good life. It does, however, underestimate the fundamental differences between Christian and secular views of the nature of ethical reasoning—differences so profound that they raise grave questions about the very possibility of describing ethics as some type of ongoing "conversation" about moral dilemmas in which many different "voices" participate.

This much becomes clear as soon as it is realized that people cannot ask "What ought I do?," without answering two preliminary and inter-related questions. These are:

- Who am I?
- What are the options to be done?

Put another way, what is the anthropological status of human beings in the reality in which they find themselves, and how does this shape and limit our moral options? If, for example, we regard human beings as simply one of a number of species, then we are likely to arrive at different answers to various ethical dilemmas than those who suppose that human life is of intrinsically greater worth than that of other creatures.

Christianity has a clear position on the nature of reality and humanity's place in it. God is the Creator, and all beings in the universe—creatures in general and humans in particular—are, therefore, considered to owe their existence to him. The essence of humanity is thus viewed as derivative from God and reflecting his eternal thoughts and plans. The dignity of human beings is expressed especially in the fact that they can understand this divine and natural order and choose to conform to it in their actions, thereby participating in the thought of God and having a share in the cosmological order that he bestowed on the world when he created it. Consequently, ethical reasoning for the Christian does not consist in people somehow creating "their own" moral order or "their own" truth. Instead, it takes the form of people attaining an ever-deepening knowledge of the unchanging truth about good and evil.

To this extent, ethics studied from a Christian vision of reality is premised on quite different foundations from the view adopted by some secular humanists. Hence, if ethics involves answering questions about the appropriateness of given acts to the given reality, it may be said that because of profoundly different understandings of human nature, it is actually more accurate to speak of "Christian ethics," "secular humanist ethics," "Buddhist ethics," and so forth, and to limit use of the word *ethics* to describe the intellectual exercise of determining what one ought to do.

Where, then, do people studying Christian ethics turn when seeking to understand the truth about human reality and to determine what people ought to do in light of such knowledge? In 1972, Pope Paul VI provided a useful summary of the distinctly Christian sources of ethical reflection when he explained the nature of Christian morality:

> We could define it precisely in an empirical way by stating that it is a way of living according to the Faith, in light of the Truths and example of Christ, such as we learned from the Gospel and from its first apostolic irradiation, the New Testament, always in view of a second coming of Christ and a new form of our existence, the so-called *Parousia*, and always by means of a double aid, one interior and one ineffable, the Holy Spirit; the other exterior, historical and social, but qualified and authorized, the ecclesiastical Magisterium.[1]

Protestants would generally take a somewhat different view because of their general emphasis on the primacy of Scripture (*sola scriptura*). Here, however, is not the appropriate place to discuss the dissimilarities between various Christian traditions on this particular subject. For our purposes, it suffices to note that a form of ethical discourse that describes itself as Christian must involve reflection upon what faith in God's revelation, culminating in the person of Jesus Christ, tells us about God, man's place in the cosmos, and the nature of the kingdom that is to come. It then involves the application of this knowledge to particular circumstances and dilemmas so as to guide and judge *each and every* free act of persons who desire to live in truth. Such reflection must acknowledge that for the Christian, there is an intrinsic and inseparable link between faith and morality, manifested in Christ's statement: "If you love me, you will keep my commandments" (Jn 14:15).

Christian ethics is not, therefore, a pragmatic endeavor. It is an exercise in identifying those acts that conform to the demands of faith and the love of God, and those acts that are incompatible with the same demands. This being the case, Christian ethics is not only about making choices for or against one or another particular action. It also involves, within the setting of that choice, making a decision for or against the truth and, ultimately, for or against God. For the Christian, the act of faith cannot be separated from the free choice of other acts. It is something to be lived out in all of one's daily decisions and actions, no matter how trivial they seem.

Paradoxes and Problems

If one reflects upon the preceding outline of the nature of Christian ethics, it soon becomes apparent why economists and Christian thinkers often talk at cross-purposes and sometimes clash directly. Three problems tend to manifest themselves.

Ignoring the Insights of Positive Economics

Medieval scholars such as Saint Albert Magnus and Saint Thomas Aquinas were among the first to state that the sciences require autonomy if they are to function properly in their respective fields of research. There is, however, a propensity for some Christians to forget this axiom when it comes to economics. In doing so, they fail to recognize that the orientations of positive economics and Christian ethics are quite different. As intellectual disciplines, the former focuses upon the *descriptive*, while the latter is *prescriptive.*

To state, for example, that there is a relationship between supply and demand or that self-interest plays a role in people's economic choices is simply to describe two characteristics of economic life. Some might even contend that to deny or ignore these realities is to deny or ignore aspects of the truth, the pursuit of which is fundamental to the Christian vision of man's destiny because, as Saint John's Gospel reminds us, "the truth will set you free" (Jn 8:32).

In this light, it is quite understandable for some economists to become frustrated by some Christians' reluctance to acknowledge the insights of positive economics or to consider the implications of such insights for the formulation of economic policy. Indeed, they correctly argue that it is irresponsible for people studying public policy from a Christian perspective to ignore not only the self-evident fact of scarcity but also the likely economic consequences of different choices. Such information can be made available only by positive economics. As Boettke observes, positive economics endows us with as close to "value-neutral" knowledge as can be furnished by a social science. This, in turn, supplies us with some of the information required for a reasoned discussion of what is the soundest choice to make,[2] not least by telling us how scarce resources may be allocated among competing ends and by presenting us with some empirical grounds for assessing which policy choices are likely to improve or worsen particular situations in material terms. Positive economics is, thus, capable of providing Christian thinkers with particular insights into what is humanly possible, and Christians who are willing to pay attention to its conclusions are less likely to find that their contributions to policy formulation amount to little more than an exercise in wishful thinking.[3]

Exaggerating the Claims of Economics

Though some Christians are often reluctant to acknowledge the insights of positive economics, economists are not guiltless when it comes to explaining the tensions that sometimes arise between them and Christian thinkers. In recent decades, some economists may have exaggerated the explanatory power of their discipline. In such instances, positive economics becomes transformed, from an intellectual discipline that studies and makes various claims about certain aspects of material reality, into what almost amounts to an ideology.

Few would deny that reflection upon the workings of economic self-interest provides us with many insights into the actions of human beings. Even fewer would dispute that there is an economic dimension to historical events such as World War I, to epochal transformations such as the Protestant Reformation, or to social institutions such as the family. Most would even agree that economic processes are often the most important thing that people must understand if they want to grasp the meaning and nature of a great number of these phenomena.

There are, however, some economists who take Adam Smith's observation that people pursue their own self-interest in the material realm and elevate it to the status of an article of faith, thereby holding that *everything* is essentially driven by economic self-interest. As noted by Nobel prize recipient James Buchanan, and his colleague, Geoffrey Brennan, some economists do seem to think and act as if "the rarefied *homo economicus* construction is, if not the perfect image of real man, at least so sufficiently close so that no great violence is done by assuming that real man is actually *homo economicus*."[4] An example of this tendency may be found in George Stigler's Harvard University Tanner Lecture, "The Economist As Preacher."[5]

Curiously, the outlook of such economists could be viewed as almost as reductionist as Marxism, which is an ideology that, broadly speaking, holds that *every* idea, institution, conviction, and event is simply a manifestation of the inevitable and ongoing class struggle throughout history for control of the means of production. As Robert Nelson—a pro-market economist—points out, these economists view noneconomic values as merely serving "to obscure the deeper workings of the forces of self-interested economic rationality."[6] This position is remarkably analogous to the Marxist thesis that the "superstructure" of culture merely reflects the deeper structure of the "class struggle." Economists who fall into the error highlighted by Nelson go far beyond Adam Smith whose reflections on self-interest in *The Wealth of Nations* (1776) should always be placed in the context of his earlier, lesser-known work, *The Theory of Moral Sentiments* (1759), which speaks of the primary, nonmaterial motivations of justice, benevolence, and prudence, of which desire for honor, respect, social advancement, and wealth are subsets. It should, therefore, come as no surprise that many Christians react negatively to what comes close to being an assertion by some economists that *homo economicus* is actually the closest approximation of human reality rather than simply an abstract intellectual tool.

Economic Evidence or Moral Principle?

It is, however, more common for economists and Christian thinkers to fall out over the respective weight that should be given to the evidence of positive economics or the imperatives of moral principle when it comes to the normative exercise of formulating and implementing economic policy. One would expect an economist working in a public policy capacity to stress what positive economics tells us about the likely effects of a particular policy. If, however, an economist acting as a policy adviser insists that this is the only criterion that should be taken into account, then he is committing the basic error of supposing that an *is* makes an *ought*. To take a fictional example, one economist's research may lead him to conclude that there is much empirical evidence to suggest that a combination of slavery and child labor is the most efficient economic system of all. This conclusion, however, does not, taken in isolation, legitimize a governmental policy of permitting the development of a slave trade or allowing people to sell themselves and their children into slavery.

But when it comes to more "real-world" economic policies, one often finds that the different philosophical premises underlying what may be described as the broadly economic and broadly Christian ways of thinking are at the root of much tension between economists and Christian ethicists. Economic thinking about policy outcomes is essentially rooted in utilitarianism, the school of ethical thought that asserts that the proper choice between any two alternatives is the one calculated to lead to the greatest amount of "utility" or "satisfaction" for humanity. The greatest incommensurability between utilitarian and Christian ethics concerns the possibility of doing evil to achieve a good result. Put in relatively simple terms, the orthodox Christian view is that evil, small or large, can *never* be done, regardless of how much good may flow from it (Rm 3:8), but harmful side effects (such as the death of innocent people where their death is not part of the plan) can, in rare circumstances, be accepted.[7] The utilitarian approach, by contrast, would hold that—providing that the good effects outweighed all the bad ones—the taking of human life is permissible.

Economists rarely deal with such life-and-death issues directly, but they do presume that the best economic policy is the one that has the best effects overall—even if it does have some bad effects. We should not be surprised, then, that the utilitarian premises of economics are likely to lead some economists to different conclusions about the precise ethical status of economic policies than those arrived at by some Christians.

But beyond philosophical considerations, it should be noted that particular difficulties arise when it comes to economic policy precisely because there is no such thing as an economic policy that will not have some harmful effects in either the short- or the long-term. The case of tariffs is a good example. Regardless of whether a government decides to retain or abolish them, some people are going to be negatively affected by its decision. Ethically speaking, the situation is further complicated by the fact that the negative and positive effects of many economic policies will not always be immediately apparent or clearly discernible because of the limited foresight that humans have into such matters.

This reality creates particular challenges for Christians when it comes to thinking about public policy. It is unreasonable for them to demand that no one in the short- or long-term should be negatively affected by some economic policies, but as the theologian and economist Daniel Finn states, "Church documents at times speak as if even relatively minor harmful side effects prevent the moral approbation of economic policies or whole economic systems."[8]

This creates a twofold challenge for Christian ethicists and church leaders seeking to make meaningful contributions to economic policy debates. They must determine what moral goods are so basic that they must be respected, even at heavy costs. Second, they should devote more effort and time to the intellectually laborious but essential task of rigorously discerning the object, intention, and side effects of economic policies so as to determine, as far as humanly possible, whether they conform to the truth about the good.

At the moment, however, Christians have no more reason to be suspicious of economics as a predictive intellectual exercise than of any of the sciences. There is, of course, a long-standing debate between the merits of faith and reason, on the one hand, and instrumental reason on the other. This debate will probably continue, notwithstanding the demonstrable dependence of the scientific enterprise—indeed, of intellectual life itself—on the heritage bequeathed by the Judeo–Christian foundations of Western civilization, but this debate has no special significance for economics. Whatever Christians make of the experiments proceeding from the "Enlightenment" (that highly prejudicial phrase that implies that the world that existed before the eighteenth century was mired in ignorance and superstition) and from science itself, they must also apply these doubts and objections to modern medicine, biology, and geology as to economics.

Christians might rightly object to economists' speaking on matters of public policy as if the economic calculus were the only legitimate basis for gauging improvements in social welfare, but they go too far when they reject that same calculus as having nothing of value to offer. Within its appointed sphere of the study of material well-being, there is, at present, no coherent alternative to economics for assessing whether particular policies are likely to improve material standards of living. The key is recognizing that good economics is not synonymous with good public policy. The latter demands attention to a wider set of criteria than the material.

If Christians believe that the political process has become excessively concerned with economic matters, it is hardly fair to blame economics or economists for this state of affairs. Politics, at least in a democracy, reflects the preferences of voters. Unless—and until—voters are prepared to support policies that trade gains in material welfare for nonmaterial objectives, including a sense of community and devotion to personal holiness, we should not be surprised that economics and economists occupy center stage in the unfolding drama.

Toward a Dialogue

Given the difficulties impeding meaningful engagement between economics and Christian ethics, one is bound to wonder how a more constructive relationship may be forged. Three broad suggestions are discussed below.

Deepening One's Understanding of Economic Models

Economic models are similar to maps. Maps provide us with insight into aspects of the truth, but they do not, in themselves, capture the whole truth. A map of London can tell us how to get from Heathrow to

Westminster, but it cannot encapsulate the whole reality of the city such as the crowds, the smog, and the inhabitants' everyday joys and disappointments. Economic models are similar in that they do not attempt to encapsulate a holistic vision of the world, but they can tell us with a high degree of accuracy how to get from point A to point B if we want to attain certain material objectives, even though they equate only to an approximation of the reality they depict. Christian thinkers should therefore be careful before accusing economists of excessive abstractness. Abstractness is often necessary if we are to reach any conclusions about how certain material and economic objectives might be attained. Buchanan and Brennan remind us that abstraction is a way "of allowing economists to impose intellectual order on the observed chaos of human interaction, without excessive distracting detail in dimensions of the analysis that are not centrally relevant."[9]

By the same token, economists should acknowledge that economic models are useful only for certain purposes and do not—and cannot—embrace the whole of reality. A London street directory will not show us the distance between New York and London, nor does it tell us that we *should* travel from Heathrow to Westminster. It merely provides us with some of the information that we may need *if* we choose to go about attaining a particular goal. Economic models perform a similar function when it comes to thinking about how certain economic objectives may be realized. They are not designed to provide us with answers to moral dilemmas.

This should not be interpreted as a call for economists to abandon the presumption of *homo economicus.* On the contrary, it merely echoes the plea of Buchanan and Brennan to their fellow economists:

> [R]ecognize that *homo economicus* has its own limits as a useful abstraction. We can only load the construction with so much, and we stand in danger of having our whole "science" collapse in an absurd heap if we push beyond the useful limits. The fact that the whole set of "noneconomic" motivations are more difficult to model than the "economic" should not lead us to deny their existence.[10]

Mutual Affirmation of Truth

In a particularly insightful reflection upon economics, faith, and the nature of truth, economist Jennifer Roback Morse stresses that, for all the obvious differences between economics and Christianity, their most significant point of contact is that each affirms that there is truth. No serious Christian would, of course, affirm that economics contains the whole truth about man and the cosmos, but economists would agree with Christians that, to cite Morse, "human nature is something universal and enduring."[11] Two fundamental truths about the human person affirmed by both economics and Christianity are:

- People have reason and are capable of freely willed acts; and
- Self-interest does play a role in human decision making.

By and large, economists do not believe that some of these facts might be true for some people but not for others. They are held to be *universally* true.

Over time, economists have applied these facts to almost every human activity imaginable. In the 1960s, for example, the Public Choice School began applying the observation that people act in their self-interest to the study of those working in the public sector. Consequently, they not only brought into question the common presumption that governmental officials typically act in the public interest—a supposition that had already been questioned, from a sociological viewpoint, by Max Weber—but also brought to light much economic evidence that suggests that many state officials have a tendency to promote their own political and economic interests to the detriment of the common good.[12] Economists have thus been successful in generating new insights into a range of problems precisely because they have focused on certain verifiable constants in human behavior.

Some social scientists do not agree with these propositions. Those who have succumbed to the current fashion of deconstructionism would generally dispute that there is even such a thing as truth, save the "truth" that "everything is relative" or that everything is explainable in Foucaultian terms of "hidden power interests," especially those of a "patriarchal" character. Others are outright determinists, believing that people are driven by social forces or "laws of history" beyond their control.

While one can accept that people are influenced by their environment, its effects upon human decision making are often vastly overstated, to the point that the reality of human agency is obscured. From a Christian perspective, one of the strengths of economics is that it does not succumb to this temptation. For although economists consider economic restraints such as income and prices as causative factors in accounting for human behavior, the very language of economics highlights the fact that the person is still an agent who makes choices. Economists say that, given the constraints of income and prices, a person chooses to produce or consume one thing rather than something else. They generally do not argue that people, even those with few resources, have no choices.

The economist's picture of man as a freely choosing, reasoning human subject of action is consistent with the insistence of Christian ethics that humanity's capacity for free choice is a reality, not an illusion. Both Yahweh in the Old Testament and Christ in the New Testament specify repeatedly that humans can choose either to do what is pleasing in God's sight (and thereby attain true freedom) or to do evil (and become slaves to sin). In short, Christians believe that people's capacity, as Lord Acton put it, to choose freely to do what they ought to do,[13] is integral to their dignity as the *imago Dei* and constitutes true freedom. Where the Christian understanding of choice differs from that of the economist is precisely the Christian linking of free choice to the *responsibility* to choose the good. Positive economics, by contrast, does not ask questions about the moral rightness or wrongness of people's choices.

Another point of convergence between the economic and Christian perspectives is the latter's acknowledgment that self-interest does play a role in human decision making. Implicit recognition of this may be found in Aquinas's discussion of why private ownership is morally licit and even necessary. First, Aquinas states, people tend to care better for what is theirs than for what is common to everyone, since individuals tend to shirk responsibilities that belong to no one in particular. Second, if everyone were responsible for everything, the result would be confusion. Third, dividing things up generally produces a more peaceful state of affairs, while sharing common things often results in tension.[14]

Underlying Aquinas's observations are several assumptions: that people are fallible; that they will be guided, to a large extent, by their personal interests in economic matters; and that it is unwise in the long term to rely upon people's altruism. Late-Scholastic thinkers associated with the School of Salamanca took these insights somewhat further, suggesting that, due to original sin, the tendency to pursue self-interest in economic affairs is part of the human condition.[15] In more recent years, theologians such as Michael Novak have explored the notion of self-interest, seeking to rescue it from being narrowly interpreted as selfishness by revisiting the doctrine of Original Sin as well as Adam Smith's and Alexis de Tocqueville's respective treatments of self-interest.[16] Even more recently, John Paul II expounded what amounts to a Christian analysis of the origin and nature of human self-interest:

[M]an, who was created for freedom, bears within himself the wound of original sin, which constantly draws him towards evil and puts him in need of redemption. Not only is *this doctrine an integral part of Christian revelation*; it also has great hermeneutical value insofar as it helps one to understand human reality. Man tends towards good, but he is also capable of evil. He can transcend his immediate interest and still remain bound to it. The social order will be all the more stable, the more it takes this fact into account and does not place in opposition personal interest and the interests of society as a whole, but rather seeks to bring them into fruitful harmony. In fact, where self-interest is violently suppressed, it is replaced by a burdensome system of bureaucratic control which dries up the wellsprings of initiative and creativity.[17]

To the extent, then, that both economists and Christian ethicists agree that people are, by nature, capable of choice and shaped, in part, by personal interest, they appear to agree that there is such a thing as a human nature that is universal and enduring. If this is the case, then such a nature can be studied systematically.

This observation may give natural-law thinking, including that of a Christian variety, a point of entry into dialogue with modern economics. Although the natural-law tradition is commonly associated with Catholic moral theology, it has also exerted major influence upon Protestant theologians such as Martin Luther and John Calvin,[18] as well as important Jewish scholars such as Moses Maimonides.[19]

In general terms, Christian natural-law thinking maintains that there is a divine order, an eternal law by which God arranges, directs, and governs everything. Unlike other creatures, humans, it suggests, are not cared for through the laws of physical nature, but, rather, "from within"—that is, through the workings of right reason (*recta ratio*), which, by its natural knowledge of God's eternal law is able to show people the right direction to take when they act freely. This participation by human beings in the eternal law is called the *natural law*,[20] a law that transcends historical and cultural settings.

Like Christian natural-law philosophy, economics holds that people *can* know truth—that is, "what is" and not simply "what I think or wish to be"—by the correct and disciplined application of human reason. Thus, within the confines of their respective focuses, economics and Christian ethics share an anti-relativist view of the world. Neither regards truth as being determined by feelings, opinion polls, or focus groups. Instead, each considers knowledge of truth to proceed from a consonance between the intellect and human reality.

Much preliminary work is required if a dialogue between economists and Christian thinkers is to proceed on this basis. Christian natural-law thinking may, however, provide a starting point. Even if such a dialogue does no more than encourage some Christian thinkers to appreciate that economists do believe that, through reason, we can know truth about wealth creation and distribution while simultaneously helping some economists to recognize that the human intellect's speculative powers can discern truths beyond the scientific and the empirical (albeit in a way that is imperfect and analogical), then it may have been worthwhile.

Knowing the Limits

By recognizing the respective disciplinary limits of economics and Christian ethics, economists and Christian ethicists will be able to play a more productive role in building up the sum of knowledge that each draws upon when contributing to public policy. In this regard, Jonathan Sacks, Chief Rabbi of Great Britain and the Commonwealth, observes:

> *Ideas and institutions that have great benefit in their own domain have disastrous consequences when they are applied to another domain.* Religion has great virtues in ordering communities. It has dire consequences when employed to govern states. Scientific method is supreme in explaining natural phenomena. It is catastrophic when used to prescribe human behavior.[21]

Operating as they do from a perspective that looks beyond the limits of science for inspiration and direction, Christian ethicists can remind economists (indeed, all social and physical scientists) of what the patristic scholar Cardinal Jean Daniélou, S.J., called "the constantly provisional character of scientific systems." As Daniélou noted, these systems are "working hypotheses designed to express the most closely approximate interpretations of a body of known facts. And the discovery of new facts always opens up the possibility of challenging them."[22]

More generally, Christian ethics can act as a corrective to those economists who mistake their knowledge of some truths about human beings as being the whole truth about man. This is particularly important if Murray Rothbard, one of the leading thinkers of the Austrian school of economics, is correct when he makes the following claim:

> In recent years, economists have invaded other intellectual disciplines and, in the dubious name of science, have employed staggeringly oversimplified assumptions in order to make sweeping and provocative

conclusions about fields they know little about. This is a modern form of "economic imperialism" in the realm of the intellect. Almost always, the bias of this economic imperialism has been quantitative and implicitly Benthamite, in which poetry and pushpin are reduced to a single-level, and which amply justifies the gibe of Oscar Wilde about cynics, that they (economists) know the price of everything and the value of nothing. The results of this economic imperialism have been particularly ludicrous in the fields of sex, the family, and education.[23]

If this is an accurate analysis, Christian thinkers can help counter such tendencies by alerting economists who are working in the realm of public policy to the noneconomic costs and benefits of economic decisions, not least in terms of sin and virtue. One would further expect Christian ethicists to focus, beyond concerns of efficiency and effectiveness, upon determining what means are appropriate to the desired ends. Often the ethical aspects of means-ends questions are not thought about fully or are not even asked by those involved in the formulation of public policy— or, even for that matter, by some Christian ethicists. Should Christians, for example, simply accept that governments may use force to redistribute wealth without continually subjecting this proposition—in each and every instance—to rigorous ethical appraisal?

How, then, can economists assist the study of Christian ethics? It is true that economic research is not going to alter basic Christian moral principles, but as Thomas Beauchamp states, while economic analysis cannot change the principle that stealing is wrong, it may help inform Christians' attitudes toward a phenomenon such as inflation, inasmuch as it provides them with a better grasp of *how* inflation arises, *why* its effects are harmful, and *what* policy choices facilitate or reduce it.[24] Positive economics can thus assist Christians in dealing with new and complex questions by identifying subtle but important implications of public policy that are not immediately apparent to those examining an issue from a predominantly moral standpoint. This, one would hope, will help Christians to engage in a more informed analysis of economic policy because it will assist them to become more conscious of the "positive" dimension of economics and more aware of the intricacies of the qualitative and quantitative effects of different economic proposals. Those who advocate policies without knowing their full range of costs and benefits are ignorant, but anyone who supports policies while knowing but not articulating these costs and benefits is simply disingenuous. Neither is an appropriate option for economists or Christian ethicists who wish to think seriously about, and shape the direction of, public policy.

The primary context for the discussion of economic policy since the collapse of communism has been that of the market economy. The very phrase *the market* makes some Christians nervous. Though often portrayed in very impersonal terms, the market is no more than the ongoing interaction of freely chosen material exchanges between human beings. Obviously, market transactions do not always facilitate just results. But before Christians dismiss it as a decidedly anti-human phenomenon, it would be useful to gain a greater appreciation of its complexity. Upon doing so, they may well come to the conclusion that, to paraphrase Winston Churchill, the market economy is the worst of all economic systems—except for all the rest.

Notes

1. Paul VI, "General Audience," *L'Osservatore Romano* (3 August 1972), 1.

2. See Boettke, "Is Economics a Moral Science?," 213.

3. It should be noted that the demands of Christian faith sometimes require Christians to perform what may seem to others to be "senseless" acts of charity, heroism, and sacrifice. Throughout the centuries, for example, countless Christians have died rather than abjure their religious beliefs. Yet, from a Christian perspective, the prospect of losing one's soul by virtue of apostatizing is senseless.

4. James Buchanan with Geoffrey Brennan, "The Normative Purpose of Economic 'Science': Rediscovery of an Eighteenth-Century Method," in *Economics: Between Predictive Science and Moral Philosophy*, ed. James Buchanan (College Station, Tex.: Texas A&M University Press, 1987), 54.

5. See George Stigler, "The Economist As Preacher" (Harvard University Tanner Lecture, 1980). For criticisms of this tendency, see R. H. Nelson, "Economic Religion Versus Christian Values," *Journal of Markets and Morality* 1, 2 (Fall 1998): 158–68.

6. Nelson, "Economic Religion Versus Christian Values," 158.

7. Here the principle of double-effect should be explained. This principle states that if an individual act has more or less two effects simultaneously, one good and one bad, I may do such an act, provided that (1) the act in itself is morally good, (2) the evil effect of the good act is not willed but only permitted or accepted, and (3) there is due proportion between the unintended evil that follows the good act, and the good achieved by that act. Aquinas uses this principle when explaining the right to self-defense (see *Summa Theologiae*, II-II, q. 64, a. 2).

8. Daniel Finn, "The Church and the Economy in the Modern World," in *Questions of Special Urgency: The Church in the Modern World Two Decades After Vatican II*, ed. J. Dwyer (Washington, D.C.: Georgetown University Press, 1986), 157.

9. Buchanan with Brennan, "The Normative Purpose," 53–54.

10. Ibid., 55.

11. Jennifer Roback Morse, "Truth and Freedom in Economic Science," in *Centesimus Annus: Assessment and Perspectives for the Future of Catholic Social Doctrine*, ed. J. P. Pham (Vatican City: Libreria Editrice Vaticana, 1998), 215.

12. See, for example, James Buchanan, R. D. Tollison, and Gordon Tullock, eds., *Toward a Theory of a Rent-Seeking Society* (College Station, Tex.: Texas A&M University Press, 1980).

13. See John Dalberg-Acton, *Selected Writings of Lord Acton*, vol. 3, *Essays in Religion, Politics, and Morality*, ed. J. R. Fears (Indianapolis: Liberty Classics, 1988), 613.

14. See *Summa Theologiae*, II-II, q. 66, a.2.

15. See Alejandro A. Chafuen, *Christians for Freedom* (San Francisco: Ignatius Press, 1986): 43–61.

16. See, for example, Michael Novak, *The Spirit of Democratic Capitalism* (New York: Simon and Schuster, 1982): 92–95.

17. John Paul II, Encyclical Letter *Centesimus Annus* (1 May 1991), no. 25. Emphasis in original.

18. See J. Budziszewski, *Written on the Heart: The Case for Natural Law* (Washington D.C.: InterVarsity Press, 1997), 207–8.

19. See David Novak, "The Mind of Maimonides," *First Things* 90 (1999): 27–33.

20. See *Summa Theologiae*, I-II, q. 91, a. 2.

21. Jonathan Sacks, *Morals and Markets* (London: Institute of Economic Affairs, 1999), 53. Emphasis in original.

22. Jean Cardinal Daniélou, S.J., *Scandaleuse Vérité* (Paris: Libraire Artheme Fayard, 1961), 3.

23. Murray Rothbard, "The Hermeneutical Invasion of Philosophy and Economics," *Review of Austrian Economics* 3 (1989): 45.

24. Thomas Beauchamp, "The Foundations of Ethics and the Foundations of Science," in *Knowing and Valuing*, vol. 4, ed. H. Engelhardt and D. Callahan (New York: Hastings Center, 1980), 260–69.

CHAPTER 4

THE INSTITUTIONAL DIMENSION: PROPERTY, RULE OF LAW, AND THE STATE

With the onset of the Great Depression in 1929, many believed that the era of the market economy had come to an end. Leaving aside the collectivist economic prescriptions then being offered by Marxist-Leninists, far more democratic figures such as the famous economist John Maynard Keynes advocated an enhanced economic role for the state, a role that went far beyond anything that had previously existed (save for the war economies of World War I).

By the 1970s, however, even the most committed Keynesian economists recognized that something was wrong. Thirty years of "pump priming" the economy (i.e., periodically increasing governmental spending) contributed not just to high rates of inflation but to a steadily growing unemployment rate in Western countries—the very misery that the planned economy was supposed to prevent. Beginning in the late 1970s, many governments decided to allow more scope for economic freedom, viewing it as part of the solution to the economic malaise of many Western countries.

In philosophical terms, the case for the market economy draws upon a number of intellectual sources for support. These include:

- the Late-Scholastics (mainly Jesuits and Dominicans) associated with the Salamanca School of the late-fifteenth and mid-seventeenth centuries;
- British classical economists such as Adam Smith; and
- the *ordo liberal* school associated with the University of Freiburg, especially convinced Christians such as the Protestant Wilhelm

Röpke and the Catholic Walter Eucken, who consciously integrated the natural-law tradition into their propositions.

Economic liberty is at the heart of the free exchange of goods and services that characterizes a market economy, but this economy also requires certain institutional features if it is to function in an efficient and just manner; the most important of these are private property, rule of law, and a limited state. If these institutional conditions did not exist, then the economy would be soon degenerate into what is commonly known as a *black market*—an economic system characterized by cheating, broken promises, and criminal behavior that serves only the interests of the strong while further marginalizing the weak.

Private Property: A Guarantor of Social Order

Nations that have developed the institution of private property have invariably been rich in material wealth, but this wealth extends also to the sciences, art, and literature. Such flourishing occurs, in part, because private property guarantees that people can rest secure, knowing that the fruits of their creative work are recognized as belonging to them. To this extent, private property helps to promote self-reliance and a certain degree of personal autonomy.

Traditionally, there have been two main philosophical defenses of private ownership. The first of these was offered by Aristotle, who argued against Plato's position that justice requires the abolition of private property. Aristotle's response was that private ownership is necessary so that people can actualize the virtues, especially liberality and magnanimity.[1] Certainly, Aristotle's response did not defend private ownership as an absolute right (and, incidentally, neither does Christianity); in fact, he recommended laws that make property private in ownership and common in use. Aristotle concluded, nevertheless, that the *polis* should respect the idea of ownership and the institution of property because it is the best way of actualizing the common use principle. A similar argument was articulated and invested with Christian meaning by Saint Thomas Aquinas.

The second justification of private property was advanced by John Locke. He agreed with Aristotle and Aquinas that the law must protect ownership by securing private property. But in contrast to Aristotle's claim that property should be protected because it serves the purpose of law (i.e., the inculcation of virtue), Locke contended that private ownership is actualized when persons mix their labor with raw materials.

While he believed that the earth, as God's gift, originally belonged to everyone in common, a person's mixing of his labor with nature conferred ownership of that material upon that person. Hence, although Locke thought that the law could assist in the often difficult task of clarifying ownership, he did not believe that law established or justified the principle itself. To illustrate his point, Locke uses the example of a person who picks a piece of fruit that does not belong to anyone else. He asks: "When does this person own the fruit?" The answer: "When the person picks it." It is rightfully his because he acquired it through expending the effort to satisfy his need. He owns property because he owns the labor expended to acquire it.[2]

A common objection to private property is that private ownership is immoral because it selfishly appropriates what was meant to be held in common. This objection, however, simply ignores the reality that private property does not in itself create a "zero-sum" situation. If one person owns property, it does not mean that another is worse off. In fact, *many* people are potentially better off when someone acquires property because the acquisition often requires productive action that is morally and materially beneficial to others. Picking a piece of fruit may simply be a matter of harvesting what God has provided in nature; growing wheat, however, where none has been grown before multiplies everyone's productive stock. Moreover, the prospect of private ownership provides people with the incentive to transform "useless" resources into productive capital, and then exchange that property in order to satisfy other unmet needs. Through this process of exchange, the original acquisition is diffused throughout the economy and becomes the possession of others. In this way, private property helps to realize the universal destination of material goods.

Another objection to private property is that its unequal distribution throughout society facilitates and maintains an inequality of wealth that, by definition, is unjust. There are several problems with this assertion. The most basic is that it contains a *non sequitur*. Inequality of wealth is *not* necessarily unfair. Christianity has always affirmed that many factors must be taken into account when thinking about what constitutes justice in the material realm. These include factors such as need, merit, willingness to take risks, the function performed by a person, and the contribution made by a person.[3]

Here we ought also to remember that private property is actually a civilizing force. One cannot exchange something unless one owns the good in the first place. By making free exchange possible, property allows us to satisfy our needs without resorting to force. Private property also makes people conscious that an affront to their neighbor's property is essentially a threat to their own property. In this way, the institution of private property makes violent transgressions against human dignity less tolerable.

The Imperative of the Rule of Law

The institution of private property in itself, however, is not enough to guarantee justice within a true market economy. Private property itself requires a given framework that enforces voluntarily agreed-upon exchanges with the force of law. Without such a guarantee, no ownership arrangement would be safe from arbitrary dissolution by other, stronger individuals. In such circumstances, a truly Darwinian-like law of the jungle would prevail.

The role of law in a market economy may be described, in very broad terms, as twofold. One is to enforce voluntary agreements to exchange goods, in the event that one or more of the parties involved decides to renege on the obligations that they have voluntarily incurred. These agreements take the form of what are widely called *contracts*. Such contracts may be simple "handshake" agreements, or they may be entered into implicitly by virtue of the fact that a voluntary exchange has occurred. This happens to each of us thousands of times in our lives. In these tacit consents, we make many promises, with the promises being inferred from the participants' actions rather than their words. An implied contract is created every time we purchase, for example, a product from the supermarket. In exchange for paying money for a good, the supermarket implicitly guarantees—provided that certain precautions are taken and the good is used properly—that such a good will not, for example, inflict a person with illness. Should a consumer find that, having followed instructions, he is made ill by the good, then he may have reason for redress against the supermarket. In such instances, both parties may resort to law to adjudicate the case.

But what if no one had any insight into what the law was likely to decide in such a case? What if the decisions made about such matters by our courts were so arbitrary and inconsistent that such predictions could not reasonably be made? What if no rules existed for courts to follow in the adjudication of such a dispute? Should any of these circumstances prevail, then the rule of law would not exist. This element of *consistency* of application is critical to the success of the market economy. Without this procedural consistency as well as the various expectations created by law, people would be hesitant to enter into voluntary exchanges. They would fear that if the exchange turns out to be based on misrepresentation by one of the contracting parties, then there would be little chance of redress in the courts.

As a result of such concerns, the phrase *rule of law* needs to be understood as involving more than the fact that a body exists to enforce contracts. It also refers to the existence of procedural consistency. When we say that the rule of law prevails, we mean:

- Rules are prospective and not retroactive, and are not in any way impossible to comply with;
- Rules are promulgated, and clear and coherent with respect to one another;
- Rules are sufficiently stable to allow people to be guided by their knowledge of the content of the rules;
- The making of decrees and orders applicable to relatively limited situations is guided by rules that are promulgated, clear, stable, and relatively general; and
- Those people who have the authority to make, administer, and apply the rules in an official capacity are accountable for their compliance with rules applicable to their performance and do actually administer the law consistently and in accordance with its tenor.

Some jurists regard adherence to rule of law as having a deterrent effect upon human behavior insofar as observance of rule of law tends to discourage individuals or organizations from doing what is illegal (even if they believe certain activities to be morally permissible) and/or otherwise widely accepted as wrong.[4] Other jurists maintain that "the rule of law, in its promulgation, prospectivity, possibility of compliance, clarity, and so forth, is best explainable in part as involving an at least minimal commitment to human dignity and responsibility."[5] As the Athenian philosophers and medieval Scholastics pointed out, rule of law involves the further "matter of doing what can be done to see that we are ruled by *reason*."[6] Law, in this sense, is the fruit of the actions of people who act according to reason rather than mere whim or passion.

From Law to the State

The importance of rule of law for ensuring that the market economy is a humane economy cannot be underestimated. The primary enforcer of the rule of law is, of course, the state, especially its executive and judicial branches. This raises the larger question of what role should be played by the state, vis-à-vis economic activity.

There are no easy answers when it comes to addressing this complex issue. The entire Christian tradition affirms that the state *does* have some role to play in economic matters, even if it is simply a question of being responsible for maintaining rule of law. Nonetheless, the Christian tradition views with alarm the claim that the state should be a heavy regulator of economic activity. How, then, are we to determine where we establish the limits to state action?

Living Subsidiarity

For some time, many Christian social thinkers have found the principle of subsidiarity, or what some Protestants call sphere sovereignty, to be helpful in providing guidance as to the parameters of state intervention in the economy.[7] Subsidiarity is, of course, a general principle; it offers no concrete policy prescriptions. As one commentator remarks:

> The application of the principle of subsidiarity is more a matter of art than of science; and, in the modern world, the principle must be applied under constantly shifting conditions. In many cases, problems that are appropriately dealt with at one level in the conditions prevailing today may be more appropriately dealt with at another level (higher or lower) in the conditions prevailing tomorrow.[8]

Inevitably, this degree of relativity means that people will disagree over the precise application of the principle to different sets of conditions. This does not, however, render it useless as a way of thinking about the state's economic role. Indeed, it helps Christians to underline the moral imperative that they should bring to any such discussion.

This imperative emerges once one begins to explore the precise meaning of subsidiarity. Its philosophical origins are to be found primarily in the natural-law tradition and Catholic social teaching. The *Catechism of the Catholic Church* explains subsidiarity in the following manner:

> A community of a higher order should not interfere in the internal life of a community of a lower order, depriving the latter of its functions, but rather should support it in case of need and help to coordinate its activity with the activities of the rest of society, always with the view to the common good.[9]

On this basis, we may contend that subsidiarity maintains that there is a distinct hierarchy for action when it comes to helping others. It effectively contains the following two guidelines:

- A community of a higher order (e.g., the state) should not interfere with the internal life of a community of a lower order (e.g., a private charity), thereby depriving the latter of its rightful functions; instead,
- Higher order communities should support lower bodies in case of need and help to coordinate their activities with the rest of society.

This joining of the rendering of assistance with the preservation of autonomy is designed to serve not only purposes of effectiveness but also certain moral ends. The family is universally recognized, for example, as the community that has primary responsibility for raising children. The state's responsibility is not to impede the exercise of this duty but, rather, to establish a coordinating framework that allows all families to *self-realize* this end. In specific instances, a parent may be manifestly incapable of caring for his child. The principle of subsidiarity would suggest that the first call of assistance for such a parent is his extended family or, failing that, a group of local parents, and—only in the absence of any other mediating institution (and as a last resort)—the state.

This example illustrates subsidiarity recognition that those most likely to be able to help people in need are those closest to them. At the same time, subsidiarity recognizes that helping people means precisely that: *assisting* them rather than completely usurping their freedom of action. Herein lies the moral lesson imparted by subsidiarity. Our capacity to act freely on the basis of reasoned choices is central to our identity as the only beings in this world capable of actualizing moral good. In rendering any assistance to others, the person being assisted must be helped to act for himself, not to become passive. Assistance that leads to dependence or passivity is contrary to the end of encouraging people to become free and responsible moral agents. This attention to the moral dimension is critical. For many faith communities, the acquisition of moral and spiritual goods is, in the final analysis, more important than one's material possessions. In such cases, the priority of the transcendent must be respected.

We see, then, that subsidiarity has important lessons for how we ought to think about the state's economic role. Clearly, subsidiarity would not allow one to conclude that the state has no role to play in the economy. In extreme cases and for short periods, there may well be a case for direct state intervention. More generally, however, it suggests that the state has an important role to play in maintaining rule of law and protecting private property, precisely because it is the state alone that has been invested with the coercive power that must necessarily support these institutions.

When we apply the principle of subsidiarity to the modern welfare state, it provides us with useful insights concerning how its violation can have negative moral and economic effects. Subsidiarity suggests that, in the first instance, a person's specific needs are first to be addressed by that individual. Should that person be unable to address his own needs, the first point of recourse consists of those closest to him. A violation of subsidiarity would, however, take place if the state were to intervene immediately before recourse was made to, for example, the family. If such direct intervention were to be adopted by the state in a systematic manner, then the following would be likely to occur:

> By intervening directly and depriving society of its responsibility, the welfare state leads to a loss of human energies and an inordinate increase of public agencies, which are dominated more by bureaucratic ways of thinking than by concern for serving their clients, and which are accompanied by an enormous increase in spending. In fact, it would appear that needs are best understood and satisfied by people who are closest to them and who act as neighbors to those in need. It should be added that certain kinds of demands often call for a response which is not simply material but which is capable of perceiving the deeper human need.[10]

In these words, John Paul II not only underscores the problem of efficiency in state welfare programs but, perhaps more important, highlights their failure to connect with the often profoundly moral and spiritual needs of the individual persons that they are designed to help.

Beyond Theory and Institutions

If we accept that economics as an intellectual discipline has much to offer Christians, are we simply to rest content with this situation? Do Christians have nothing to say about the nature of economics? It is essentially in the realm of normative economics that one finds economists emphasizing the importance of institutions such as private property and rule of law while also theorizing about the state's economic role. Given its normative nature, Christians should not be afraid to contribute to this discussion, not least because, as our final chapter illustrates, it is one of the most appropriate places for Christians to question economists.

Notes

1. See Aristotle, *The Politics of Aristotle*, ed. and trans. Ernest Barker (New York: Oxford University Press, 1958).

2. See John Locke, *Two Treatises of Government*, ed. P. Lastlett (Cambridge: Cambridge University Press, 1988), Second Treatise, sections 23, 27, 135, 137.

3. A summary of the components of distributive justice may be found in John Finnis, *Natural Law and Natural Rights* (Oxford: Clarendon Press, 1993), 173–77.

4. See Joseph Raz, *The Authority of Law* (Oxford: Clarendon Press, 1979), 223–25.

5. R. George Wright, "Does Positivism Matter?" in *The Autonomy of Law: Essays on Legal Positivism*, ed. Robert P. George (Oxford: Oxford University Press, 1996), 63.

6. John Finnis, *Aquinas: Moral, Political, and Legal Theory* (Oxford: Oxford University Press, 1998), 250.

7. For reasons of clarity, we focus here on subsidiarity. For detailed explanations of the Reformed concept of sphere sovereignty, see Abraham Kuyper, *Lectures on Calvinism* (Grand Rapids, Mich.: Eerdmans Publishing Company, 1931), chapter 3, "Calvinism and Politics"; "Sphere Sovereignty," in *Abraham Kuyper: A Centennial Reader*, ed. J. D. Bratt (Grand Rapids, Mich.: Eerdmans Publishing Company, 1998); and Elaine Storkey, "Sphere Sovereignty and the Anglo-American Tradition," in *Religion, Pluralism, and Public Life: Abraham Kuyper's Legacy for the Twenty-First Century*, ed. L. E. Lugo (Grand Rapids, Mich.: Eerdmans Publishing Company, 2000).

8. George, "Natural Law and International Order," 240.

9. *Catechism of the Catholic Church* (Mahwah, N.J.: Paulist Press, 1994), no. 1883.

10. John Paul II, *Centesimus Annus*, no. 48. This principle was first formally expounded in Catholic social teaching in Pius XI, Encyclical Letter *Quadragesimo Anno* (15 May 1931), nos. 79–80.

CHAPTER 5

QUESTIONS FOR ECONOMICS

While economics does not reside at the core of the Christian faith, it is a subject that future ministers of the Gospel should not ignore. But neither should we presume that sound economics is the universal elixir for all the problems that plague the social order. There are important and legitimate questions that Christians can and should pose to economics and the economics profession on a regular basis, especially when it comes to public policy and equity issues.

Economics and Public Policy

In more recent decades, economists have assumed a more prominent role when it comes to the question of formulating public policy not only at the level of regional and national governments but also in international institutions. Given the necessary narrowness of economics as a discipline, this concerns many people. Why, it is asked, should we pay so much heed to the insights of a discipline that is, by definition, profoundly materialistic in its orientation and foundational premises?

On one level, such a concern is justified. Any government that would make decisions based purely on economic analysis would hardly be paying due regard to the complexity of human life. Nevertheless, it is important for Christians to remember that, as an intellectual discipline, economics teaches us how to generate maximum material wealth from a limited supply of material resources. Whether this is a morally defensible activity is not a question that economics seeks to answer. Economists spend much of their time studying the problem of *economic efficiency*: the problem of how best to allocate the world's scarce sources of land, labor, capital,

47

and enterprise among an unlimited number of competing alternative uses. An efficient allocation is one that generates maximum satisfaction for consumers who are assumed to be clones of *homo economicus*. In other words, the quest for efficiency is the quest for maximum material well-being, since this is all that *homo economicus* values.

If we think of economics as the discipline of material wealth creation, we cast it in its proper light as a "utilitarian" discipline such as engineering or dentistry. Like engineers and dentists, it is the task of economists to advise on how best to achieve certain specified objectives, not to judge the ultimate worth of the objectives themselves. Thus, good engineers design and build bridges that stand up; they enjoy no competence *qua* engineer to judge the value of the bridge to society. Likewise, the good economist advises on measures that will increase or decrease the level of material well-being, but he makes no presumption to knowledge of whether people are better off, in the most general sense, as a result.

Economists who exceed their mandate do the discipline a great disservice. Responsible economists are those who offer advice, when asked, on how to achieve specific objectives at minimal cost. This ensures maximum material benefit. Of course, an economist may or may not agree that the specific objectives are worthy of achievement, and economics in itself provides no moral basis upon which to make such a judgment. But as individuals—and, certainly, if they are Christians—economists may form a view of the worth of the ultimate objectives they are asked to realize. There may well be occasions that an economist, *as a person*, may feel so offended by the objective in view that he declines to offer professional economic advice. In the same way, an engineer may refuse to design and build an efficient gas chamber, or a doctor may refuse to terminate an unborn child's life.

While economists are sometimes guilty of using their status as scientists to confer legitimacy upon purely normative judgments, they do not do so as often as it may seem to the layperson. The appearance of preaching is often the result of a lamentable looseness of phraseology. A common claim of economists is that "university openings should be allocated on the basis of user-pays." Some economists may well support the application of the user-pays principle in higher education on purely political grounds. But the majority are simply stating a more carefully worded proposition that can be demonstrated empirically: "If the objective is to maximize the economic efficiency with which higher education services are produced and allocated to consumers, fees should be charged for access to higher education." It remains, however, that loosely worded claims by economists convey the impression of arrogance and partiality and bring economics into disrepute.

Public disdain of economists is often less the result of some economists' habit of lecturing on public policy than a result of confusion over the objectives of policy. Some people object to economists' call for free trade on the grounds that those working in protected industries may lose their jobs if tariffs or other protective devices are removed. Jobs, they posit, should be protected at the expense of economic growth.

But economists point out that employment growth and material progress are consistent, not contradictory, objectives. Even if the objectives were couched specifically in terms of protecting a given number of jobs, most economists would still advocate the abolition of import protection. The resources released from inefficient protected industries are then free to be reallocated toward more efficient industries that can compete in the international marketplace without assistance. More competitive industries employ more labor, resulting in more, rather than fewer, jobs. Empirical evidence shows that import protection is, in any case, an ineffective means of protecting employment. Protected industries eventually shed jobs, as they fall further behind in the competitive race.

Economics and Equity

Another reason that many people hold economics in low regard is the perception that the discipline largely ignores questions of fairness or equity. Here the perception of the lay observer is largely correct. Economics as a discipline does not concern itself with such issues.

The failure to address equity issues is not, however, due to the fact that economists think the issue is unimportant. Economics can tell us how wealth is created and how, once created, it is distributed; but it is powerless to tell us how wealth *should* be distributed, at least not without explicit information about how much people value their material wealth. In any given society, there will be as many opinions about this as there are people.

Yet, while economists can say little, if anything, about the optimal distribution of wealth, they *can* say a good deal about the costs of achieving particular wealth distributions. The distribution of the end product of economic activity—that is, material income and wealth—is strongly influenced by the distribution of the ownership of basic resources. If someone owns a great deal of land and capital or, alternatively, is gifted with some rare and highly prized talent (such as a beautiful singing voice), it usually follows that such a person is richly rewarded by the market system. If the distribution of basic resources—land, labor, capital, and entrepreneurial ability—follows a particular pattern, the distribution of income and wealth will follow much the same pattern.

The distribution of the fruits of economic creativity is something about which people often strongly disagree. Many have a vision of the ideal distribution of income and wealth that differs markedly from what a market economy produces. This leads them to advocate intervention in the economic system, with the express intention of altering the outcome. While economists are in no position to tell a government that its view of the ideal income distribution is inferior (or superior, for that matter) to what the economy would produce by itself, they do have much to say about the material *costs* of attempting to interfere with economic activity so as to influence deliberately the pattern of income distribution.

Economics tells us that changing the distribution of the fruits of economic activity is a costly business. Generally, the distribution can be changed only through the imposition of taxes, subsidies, or regulations of one sort or another. Much theoretical and empirical work by economists shows how severely interventions of this sort can affect the wealth-creating ability of an economic system. This is the economic cost of governmental intervention, realized in terms of a slower overall rate of economic growth. For reasons that economists can explain with some confidence, attempts by governments to alter the sizes of the individual slices of the economic pie tend to reduce the size of the pie itself, or at least prevent it from expanding as quickly as it might have otherwise.

It is this observation, well-established in theory and in fact, that underlies most economists' belief that economic growth is the surest way to improve the material fortunes of those at the bottom end of the income and wealth distribution scheme. The best way to achieve some increase in the size of the smallest slices is to make the whole pie bigger. A rising (economic) tide lifts all boats.

Some people interpret this claim as a prejudice on the part of economists in favor of economic growth for its own sake and against any kind of redistributive intervention by governments. While this may describe the personal opinions of some economists, it finds no warrant in the logic of economic analysis. Economics merely points to the trade-off that exists between efficiency and equity—between the desire to have more of all goods and services and the desire to see them distributed differently. It illustrates that if we want a different income distribution, it will cost us something—perhaps a great deal—in terms of foregone material improvement for society as a whole. A better idea may be to leave the income distribution the way it is and concentrate on improving the absolute material conditions of people across the income spectrum through higher rates of economic growth.

None of this is to say that income redistribution should not be attempted or that economic growth should never be sacrificed in favor of a more equitable distribution of income. Economics cannot prove that it is wrong to pursue such a course, but it can highlight the material costs and benefits to different groups of people and help them to make up their minds as to whether they will be better off as a result.

Economics and the Free Market

Another concern related to the question of equity is the concept that economics as a discipline is blind to the pitfalls of the market mechanism. This is not entirely true. There have been many economists who have advocated state-planned or even collectivist economic systems because they believed that a planned system would be more efficient than a free market at producing and distributing goods. Now, however, we have a substantial body of empirical evidence that favors the free market as a more efficient means of creating material wealth than any other economic system yet devised. Contemporary economists' support of the free market is based more upon their acceptance of this evidence than upon mere ideological prejudice. To an economist (or, indeed, to anyone who has observed the evidence), the statement that the market is inferior as a device for creating material wealth in comparison, for instance, to Soviet-style central planning has as much empirical credibility as the statement that the earth is flat.

This is not to say that all economists are blind to the failures of the market, not least because the more perceptive recognize that the market is driven by an economic calculus rather than by moral imperatives, and that this will sometimes cause problems. The market will create wealth with equal ease through the prostitution of women and children as it will through the design and manufacture of life-saving medical equipment. For this reason, many economists have acknowledged the need to place the market economy within a framework of law and upon a particular moral and cultural foundation. Many economists even hold that the market, while superior to all other economic systems, is nevertheless flawed, and they will recommend alternative mechanisms for wealth creation and/or distribution if a sound case can be made. A case is *not*, however, established just by showing the market to be defective. Economists' studies of alternative allocation devices, including government central planning or administrative fiat, reveal weaknesses with these approaches as well. The case for replacing the market mechanism with some alternative allocation scheme must rest upon proof that the costs incurred by departing from free-market principles are not, in fact, *greater* than the costs of staying with the market solution, imperfect though it is.

To this extent, economists have a "rational prejudice" for market solutions as devices for creating material wealth based upon demonstrable scientific evidence, but their standards of academic integrity demand that alternative solutions be sought and considered if the market fails to deliver maximum economic efficiency.

While the principle of the matter is clear—in this area more than any other—economists allow their own political preferences to sway their judgment, especially in public forums. The appropriate extent of governmental intervention in economic affairs is an issue that divides economists as no other. On this issue, the spectrum of professional opinion reflects the spectrum within the general community, which immediately gives rise to the suspicion that political preference holds sway over empirical observation. The evidence, both theoretical and empirical, reveals a much narrower range of opinion than is widely professed. It follows that economists are to be questioned most closely when they are defending a departure from competitive market solutions in favor of an interventionist model. The "presumption of innocence" favors the market, and, while it is far from infallible, the market's guilt needs to be established beyond reasonable doubt before sentence is passed.

It should also be acknowledged that in more recent times, economists have turned their attention to goods that do not enter into market exchange and that, therefore, tend to be undersupplied. In doing so, economists have taken economic methods into previously uncharted waters and, in doing so, have advanced proposals likely to enhance the common good. The prime example is environmental amenity, including the claimed right to breathe unpolluted air and to swim in unpolluted waters. These are "goods" for which there has traditionally been no market. In analyzing the problem of environmental pollution, economists such as Nobel prize winner Ronald Coase have employed their understanding of the market mechanism to explain why the problem arises and to suggest remedies. Economists know from theory and experience that the market is a powerful engine and can be harnessed to achieve profound change. By designing mechanisms through which market forces are brought to bear on pollution, such as creating tradable pollution rights, economists have assisted governments to manage a problem that excites substantial public concern. This and other developments in the application of economic insights to problems that deeply concern humanity ought to strike a positive chord with Christians anxious to see public policy enhance those conditions that allow all humans to fulfill themselves as persons more easily.

Economics As Faith

The example of the application of market-orientated solutions to new problems facing humanity should not, however, blind us to the wisdom of the axiom: "Economic models are to be used, not to be believed." This demonstrates the tentative nature of all scientific knowledge, but it also warns us against taking the conclusions of economic analysis as articles of faith. Economics attempts to understand the material world. It does not promulgate a philosophy of life, much less a set of metaphysical values by which people might attempt to live worthwhile lives. Economics is not a religion.

Yet some economists have certainly fallen into this trap. Some actually believe that *homo economicus* is the closest abstract approximation of the human person that the secular mind has yet formulated. Both faith and practical reason, however, tell the Christian that such claims are simply not true. Each person can certainly make himself into Hobbesian man as a result of his free choices and actions. But this is far from the only alternative.

Economists are not alone, of course, in allowing their technical knowledge to assume the status of Holy Writ. Some scientists also occasionally display intellectual arrogance, convinced that no possible turn of events could falsify their firmly held beliefs. Such behavior is as unbecoming as it is unscientific, yet it is the practitioner of science, rather than science itself, who bears the fault. Likewise, it is economists, rather than economics, who should be judged when the tentative conclusions of their analyses are presented to the lay public as eternal truths.

But what should perhaps be of even greater concern to Christians is the large number of economists and those studying economics who have never examined the philosophical validity of the utilitarianism that underlies the methods and models of economics. As serious Christians recognize, utilitarianism and its most contemporary manifestation, consequentialism, are deeply flawed models for moral and philosophical reasoning. Right reason itself tells us that this is true.[1]

The word *consequentialism* is normally used to refer to a moral outlook that evaluates actions or behavior according to the consequences of that behavior. According to consequentialists, the master principle of good moral acts is to direct the chooser to act in ways that are most likely to produce the best net proportion of good to bad consequences over the long-term.

The actions of individuals and groups do have consequences, and it would be morally negligent not to think about their effects. But consideration of consequences is not sufficient for judging the moral goodness or evil of a concrete free choice. Put simply, the "weighing" of the foreseeable goods and evils that proceed from an action is not an adequate method for determining whether such an action is morally good or bad. As a general strategy of moral reasoning, consequentialism is, strictly speaking, irrational. Consequentialists[2] claim:

- One should always choose the act that, so far as one can see, will yield the greatest net good on the whole and in the long run (*act utilitarianism*); or
- One should always choose according to a principle or rule, the adoption of which will yield the greatest net good on the whole and in the long run (*rule utilitarianism*).

The essential problem with these propositions is that the injunction to "maximize" moral good is senseless.[3] It presumes that the realizations of human good (and evil) are commensurable in a way that makes possible an intelligent weighing or measuring of "value."[4] Consequentialist reasoning thus relies upon the assumption that we can measure moral goods according to some single, well-defined goal or function (a dominant end).

We know, however, that when people act, they do *not* have a single common factor in mind. There is, therefore, no measuring basis against which we can somehow "weigh" the significance of various goods. But equally erroneous is the implicit consequentialist assumption that every human desire has the same *prima facie* entitlement to consideration when the "measuring" occurs. There is no reason, for example, to treat the desire of someone who wishes to keep people ignorant as a wish entitled to just as much satisfaction as the desire of someone who loves knowledge and wants others to share in knowledge.

In light of these problems, one should not be surprised that consequentialism is essentially characterized by arbitrariness. It provides, for example, no reason for preferring altruism to egoism. Jeremy Bentham, the founder of utilitarianism, equivocated and oscillated for over sixty years about whether his utilitarianism sought to maximize his own happiness or the happiness of everybody. As John Finnis remarks: "A genuinely consequentialist assessment of alternative possibilities could never end, and could begin anywhere."[5] This suggests that it should never begin at all.

Many economists, especially those who are also Christian, recognize that economics' implicit reliance on utilitarian-consequentialist assumptions is a problem the economics profession has yet to confront.[6] For those economists who are materialists, of course, there is no problem to confront, precisely because utilitarianism—with its deliberate eschewal of notions such as the transcendent, the virtues, and the basic moral goods—is essentially a philosophical manifestation of a materialist mindset, or at least, the tendency to believe that God is easily satisfied with human conduct or effortlessly appeased or bought off. Plato referred to this as one of the three varieties of practical atheism.[7]

The ultimate challenge, then, for Christians, economists who are Christians, and economists wary of utilitarianism's distinctly materialist character and philosophical incoherence, is not to attempt somehow to prove that economics has nothing to teach us. The preceding chapters illustrate that this would be a futile exercise. There is much that economics *can* teach Christians and the modern world. Instead, the intellectual task that lies before us is to explore the potential for grounding economics as a discipline in a more adequate anthropology of the human person than *homo economicus*. Rather than simply assuming that people are nothing more than utility maximizers, we have yet to discover the extent to which economics would benefit from being grounded not in an abstraction but, rather, in a full vision of man as a creature uniquely graced with free will, capable of knowing truth (both metaphysical and material) through reason, endowed with unique creative powers, and able to choose freely to do what he ought rather than simply what he feels like doing. As a discipline, economics, with its current assumptions, provides us with certain valuable insights into the truth while simultaneously eschewing the contemporary moral-cultural disease of emotivism[8] that dominates both the academy and popular culture. One wonders how much more that economics could reveal to us if its assumptions were enriched by the vision of the human person bequeathed to the world by the God who became man: Jesus Christ.

Notes

1. For a short but devastating critique of utilitarianism in its various guises (particularly that of John Stuart Mill), see Budziszewski, *Written on the Heart*, 136–67.

2. See, for example, Richard McCormick, S.J., "Ambiguity in Moral Choice," in *Doing Evil to Achieve Good*, eds. Richard McCormick, S.J., and Paul Ramsey (Lanham, Md.: University Press of America, 1978), 84–86.

3. See John Finnis, Joseph Boyle, and Germain Grisez, "Incoherence and Consequentialism (or Proportionalism): A Rejoinder," *American Catholic Philosophical Quarterly* 64 (1990): 271–72.

4. Germain Grisez, "Against Consequentialism," *American Journal of Jurisprudence* 23 (1978): 21–24.

5. Finnis, *Natural Law*, 117.

6. See, for example, Paul Cleveland, "Economic Behavior: An Inherent Problem With Utilitarianism," *Journal of Private Enterprise* (Fall 2000): 81–97

7. See Plato, *The Laws* (Harmondsworth, U.K.: Penguin Classics, 1970), 885b, 888c, 901d, 902e–903a, 908b–d, 909a–b.

8. For an exposition of the nature of the problems of emotivism, see Alasdair MacIntyre, *After Virtue: A Study in Moral Theory* (Notre Dame: Notre Dame University Press, 1981), 1–34.

Part II

INTRODUCTION

The foundations of economic theory presented in Part I of this work did not originate with me. The principles of a free economy have been slowly developing for centuries. However, economics as a formal science did not begin until the end of the eighteenth century. The modern science of economics, in large part, owes its origin to moral theology. Aristotle offered several chapters on "household management" in his *Nicomachean Ethics*, the Greek term for the subject being *oikonomiké*. Various theologians of the early Christian Church, such as Clement of Alexandria, Basil the Great, Gregory of Nazianzus, John of Chrysostom, and Augustine, were concerned with the uses and abuses of wealth, the nature and origin of private property, and issues related to proper fiscal responsibility and stewardship. Even the Scholastic theologians of the Late-Medieval period carefully reflected upon such issues as the morality of trade, the determination of economic value, the justice of prices and wages, and the state's proper role in the realm of commerce.

The Late-Scholastic theologians of the Spanish School of Salamanca deserve special attention because they developed sophisticated economic analysis that foreshadowed the work of the early modern economists, particularly on the topics of economic value, money, and prices. Adam Smith, the author of the seminal *Wealth of Nations* (1776) was primarily a moral philosopher whose other lesser-known work, *The Theory of Moral Sentiments* (1759), served as the philosophical and moral foundation of his economic theory. Economics did not come into its own as a separate and officially recognized academic discipline until the mid-nineteenth century.

What follows in this portion of the book are key selections drawn from classic economic texts with brief introductions systematically arranged around the following themes: property, trade, intervention, value and price theories, definitions of economics, wages, money, mutually beneficial exchange, marginal utility, unintended consequences, profit, supply and demand, division of labor, and taxes. Each theme, which will be introduced in turn by a one-page analytical description, has been chosen to complement and reinforce the argument of Part I. These are, then, the pivotal insights of noted economists and theologians on fundamental economic issues.

Not every classical text could be included or classical author covered in this survey. Many economists and Christian social thinkers and theologians did not find their way into this survey. Limited space does not permit such a thorough survey—other works exist that already serve this function, and the inclusion of many texts on each theme was deemed unnecessary. Therefore, our choice of selections is not meant to be interpreted as comprehensive or exhaustive of the literature on either economics or Christian social thought. Rather, the selections that comprise Part II were carefully chosen to reinforce the material presented in Part I of this work. Not only do these selections serve to reinforce the themes of Part I, but they also take the reader further into the economic way of thinking, laying out arguments and analysis concerning central economic principles and terms, and in many cases, supplying insightful applications of the concepts involved.

These selections will enable a fuller understanding of the issues at stake in the debates from many of the key participants themselves. So, take a moment to thumb through these selections and become familiar with the arguments of the great economic thinkers of the past and present. You may be struck by the common-sense, down-to-earth approach of many of the selections. Notice how the complicated mathematical formulas and intricate graphs and charts of contemporary economics are strangely absent from most of these selections. What is evident, however, is that many of the great historical economic thinkers were practitioners who keenly observed human behavior and then tried to explain the order and operation of the market. What may also be surprising to you is the overt moral tone and ethical concern of many of the authors. Many of these classic thinkers understood the principal function of their discipline to be that of serving humankind. These thinkers were each involved in the pursuit of the humane economy—one that respects human freedom while harnessing human potential in order to provide a standard of living in accord with human dignity.

SELECTED READINGS IN MORALITY AND ECONOMICS

DEFINITION OF ECONOMICS

Economics is usually understood as the discipline that studies the production, distribution, and consumption of material goods and services. Yet it might accurately be said that economics is the study of trade. Economics seeks to explain human behavior when making choices regarding the trade (or exchange) of material goods and services. Individuals, groups, businesses, and governments (among others) are all actors in the economic world. Economics explores the decisions and rationality displayed by these entities as they strive toward efficiently meeting their goals of trade.

Two major divisions in the field are micro- and macroeconomics. Microeconomics concentrates on the rational decisions made by individuals, groups, and businesses, which are trying to maximize their utility though trade. Microeconomics draws heavily from the supply and demand relationship to predict how people will act (trade) under different circumstances. Attitudes toward price and utility are important components of microeconomic analysis.

Macroeconomics deals with predicting the actions and trends of long-term business actors and governments. Large-scale players such as these often emphasize factors different from those important in the microeconomic world, for example, investment and employment. Supply and demand are still important, but they are used as aggregates compiled within the same country or actor.

Leading thinkers from the microeconomic free-market tradition include Adam Smith and David Ricardo. Smith's ideas are the basis for much of what we today call free-market economics. Ricardo also hailed from the classical school, defending the principles of private property, minimal government intervention, and the supremacy of consumer preferences.

The macroeconomic branch has been most powerfully influenced by John Maynard Keynes. Keynesian thought is still applied to many government economic decisions today. Keynes argued that the causes of unemployment were a result of decreased aggregate demand. He also asserted that business or government spending was necessary to alleviate unemployment, a concept that still carries public policy weight.

Economics has become a major study in several fields, such as psychology, ethics, business, politics, and sociology. Ultimately, human behavior is central in these areas of study as well, and so an economic component cannot be radically separated from these other disciplines.

Frank Knight (1885–1972), one of the founders of the Chicago school of economics, offers us his definition of economics. One of the more notable aspects of this definition is his use of the term *human science*. Modern economic methodology has largely been patterned after the mathematical and quantitatively based sciences. As a result, some scholars contend that economics has become inaccessible to the ordinary person. Given this trend, Knight's definition of the discipline is particularly interesting. The following selection was taken from Knight's *Risk, Uncertainty and Profit* (1964).

◆ ◆ ◆

Economics is a human science; its foundations are laid in the principles of human behavior, and consequently we must begin with some observations on the psychology of human conduct which controls economic life. Economic analysis may be truly said to deal with "conduct," in the Spencerian sense of acts adapted to ends, or of the adaptation of acts to ends, in contrast with the broader category of "behavior" in general. It assumes that men's acts are ruled by conscious motives; that, as it is more ordinarily expressed, they are directed toward the "satisfaction of wants." At the very outset the science is thus subjected to notable restrictions, since it is only to a limited extent that our behavior, even our economic behavior, is of this character. Much of it is more or less impulsive and capricious. The conclusions of economic theory must in general be admitted subject to the qualification, insofar as men's economic activities are rational or planned....

... The basis of a *science* of conduct must be fixed principles of action, enduring and stable motives. It is doubtful, however, whether this is fundamentally the character of human life. What men want is not so much to get things that they want but to have interesting experiences. And the fact seems to be that an important condition of our interest in things is an element of the unanticipated, of novelty, of surprise....

Economics, as we have observed before, is the science of a certain form of organization of human activities. The fact of organization still further limits the scope of the discussion to the rationalistic view of activity as directed to the satisfaction of wants conceived as given and permanent entities. Conduct itself is necessarily forward-looking, but organized conduct is still more so. Any machinery of organization implies relatively much taking thought, since it requires time for its development and time for its operation. A most essential feature of economic organization as it exists is its anticipation of the wants of the consumer over a long and ever longer period of production; and this anticipation implies stability in the character of the wants themselves.

The Austrian economist, **Ludwig von Mises (1881–1973)**, spent a great deal of time analyzing the philosophical and methodological foundations of economics. His central conclusion was that economics is the study of free human action. In the following selection, taken from his magnum opus *Human Action* (1949) he delineates the scope of economics.

♦ ♦ ♦

There have never been any doubts and uncertainties about the scope of economic science. Ever since people have been eager for a systematic study of economics or political economy, all have agreed that it is the task of this branch of knowledge to investigate the market phenomena, that is, the determination of the mutual exchange ratios of the goods and services negotiated on markets, their origin in human action, and their effects upon later action. The intricacy of a precise definition of the scope of economics does not stem from uncertainty with regard to the orbit of the phenomena to be investigated. It is due to the fact that the attempts to elucidate the phenomena concerned must go beyond the range of the market and of market transactions. In order to conceive the market fully, one is forced to study the action of hypothetical, isolated individuals on the one hand, and to contrast the market system with an imaginary socialist commonwealth on the other hand. In studying interpersonal exchange, one cannot avoid dealing with autistic exchange. But then it is no longer possible to define neatly the boundaries between the kind of action which is the proper field of economic science in the narrower sense, and other action. Economics widens its horizon and turns into a general science of all and every human action, into praxeology. The question emerges of how to distinguish precisely, within the broader field of praxeology, a narrower orbit of specifically economic problems....

... All that can be contended is this: Economics is mainly concerned with the analysis of the determination of money prices of goods and services exchanged on the market. In order to accomplish this task it must start from a comprehensive theory of human action. Moreover, it must study not only the market phenomena, but no less the hypothetical conduct of an isolated man and of a socialist community. Finally, it must not restrict its investigations to those modes of action which in mundane speech are called "economic" actions, but must deal also with actions which are in a loose manner of speech called "noneconomic."

Economist **Henry Hazlitt (1894–1993)** outlines the essential marks of good economic practice and deplores the neglect of the same by many "public economists" of the present. Hazlitt's clean style renders the basics of economics intelligible to a general audience in his *Economics in One Lesson* (1962).

♦ ♦ ♦

In this lies the whole difference between good economics and bad. The bad economist sees only what immediately strikes the eye; the good economist also looks beyond. The bad economist sees only the direct consequences of a proposed course; the good economist looks also at the longer and indirect consequences. The bad economist sees only what the effect of a given policy has been or will be on one particular group; the good economist inquires also what the effect of the policy will be on all groups.

The distinction may seem obvious. The precaution of looking for all the consequences of a given policy to everyone may seem elementary. Doesn't everybody know, in his personal life, that there are all sorts of indulgences delightful at the moment but disastrous in the end? Doesn't every little boy know that if he eats enough candy he will get sick? Doesn't the fellow who gets drunk know that he will wake up the next morning with a ghastly stomach and a horrible head?... Finally, to bring it to the economic though still personal realm, do not the idler and the spendthrift know, even in the midst of their glorious fling, that they are heading for a future of debt and poverty?

Yet when we enter the field of public economics, these elementary truths are ignored. There are men regarded today as brilliant economists, who deprecate saving and recommend squandering on a national scale as the way of economic salvation; and when anyone points to what the consequences of these policies will be in the long run, they reply flippantly, as might the prodigal son of a warning father: "In the long run we are all dead." And such shallow wisecracks pass as devastating epigrams and the ripest wisdom.

But the tragedy is that, on the contrary, we are already suffering the long-run consequences of the policies of the remote or recent past. Today is already the tomorrow which the bad economist yesterday urged us to ignore. The long-run consequences of some economic policies may become evident in a few months. Others may not become evident for several years. Still others may not become evident for decades. But in every case those long-run consequences are contained in the policy as surely as the hen was in the egg, the flower in the seed.

From this aspect, therefore, the whole of economics can be reduced to a single lesson, and that lesson can be reduced to a single sentence. *The art of economics consists in looking not merely at the immediate but at the longer effects of any act or policy; it consists in tracing the consequences of that policy not merely for one group but for all groups.*

PROPERTY

The concept of "property" is one of the driving forces behind free-market economics. Property defines the ownership of something by somebody or some group. Since free-market economics is founded on the trading of goods and services for purposes of self-benefit, property is essential in establishing what may be traded and by whom.

Private property is an extension of human freedom. Human nature affirms that ownership is a right of free persons. Thus, property is not only necessary for survival but also an extension of human subjectivity in the material order. Though the economic concept of private property most likely originated in ancient times, it attained a central place in economic understanding only with the rise of European mercantilism and the work of Adam Smith. The mercantilists, who depended on trade for their livelihoods, advanced the concept of property by making materials available for sale to consumers. Property is a central component of every economic system. Economics is based on the concept of trade, and the exchange of property constitutes trade.

Prior to this time, the feudal lords of Europe generally claimed all land as their own and merely allowed public use. As the medieval era passed and Smith's thought was circulated, more individuals aspired to attain ownership of property for private use.

Property implies ownership, which can mean more than simply possessing an object. Ownership also includes rights of full use over an object. One should be able to utilize their property, although, from a Christian perspective, the use of private property should always be with a mind for the universal destination of material goods. In ideal circumstances, government sanctions exist to enforce and protect the private ownership of property.

Property can be physical objects or ideas. "Real property" is most often associated with the ownership of land or structures affixed to land.

69

"Intellectual property" describes creative ideas attributed to an individual or group that can be used to their financial benefit. Examples of intellectual property are patents and copyrights.

A free-market system recognizes individuals' rights to attain property and use it as the owner sees fit. The simplest example today is of a consumer purchasing a product from a merchandiser. That product is property of the merchandiser until it is sold to the consumer. Until that time, the merchandiser may use the product as she sees fit; in this example it is beneficial to the merchandiser to sell the product and collect the consumer's money for the exchange. The consumer, now the owner of the product, may use, sell, give away, or hide the product as she desires, exercising the rights to property.

In socialist or statist systems, the rights to individual property are restricted, and the ownership rights rest more with the state. The state controls the production material and facilities as well as the distribution of many consumer products. The government also controls real property. In these systems, the state has the authority to decide which goods are most beneficial to people and allocates them using some type of formula. Of course, once allocated, these goods are, for the time being, the property of individuals, but it is important to note that in statist systems, the goal of ownership for individuals is nearly nonexistent because the state owns most everything and exercises its right of property by "giving" goods to the citizenry.

There do exist some goods or rights that may be described as "public property," even in free-market systems. Often, these are "goods" in which one person's use does not deplete another's ability to use that "good." Examples include the air we breathe and certain common goods shared and protected by a nation, such as national defense or the innocence of children. These goods in a sense are the property of everyone within the state, no matter what economic system that nation practices.

Frederic Bastiat (1801–1850), a French economist and social thinker, explains the natural tendency of human beings to grasp at the property of others. According to Bastiat, envy is a common human affliction. Less virtuous individuals choose to steal the property of others rather than exert the labor and time necessary to earn property of their own. This passage on plunder, to use Bastiat's term, comes from *The Law*, his classic work on the right use of governmental force.

♦ ♦ ♦

Man can live and satisfy his wants only by ceaseless labor; by the ceaseless application of his faculties to natural resources. This process is the origin of property.

But it is also true that a man may live and satisfy his wants by seizing and consuming the products of the labor of others. This process is the origin of plunder.

Now since man is naturally inclined to avoid pain—and since labor is pain in itself—it follows that men will resort to plunder whenever plunder is easier than work. History shows this quite clearly. And under these conditions, neither religion nor morality can stop it.

When, then, does plunder stop? It stops when it becomes more painful and more dangerous than labor.

It is evident, then, that the proper purpose of law is to use the power of its collective force to stop this fatal tendency to plunder instead of to work. All the measures of the law should protect property and punish plunder.

But, generally, the law is made by one man or one class of men. And since law cannot operate without the sanction and support of dominating force, this force must be entrusted to those who make the laws.

The following selection from **Saint Thomas Aquinas (1226–1274)** provides a classic Christian rationale for private ownership. Ownership, under this definition, is merely an extension of the freedom of the person—a necessary extension required for successful navigation through life. Property is one way that virtue may be cultivated through the practices of stewardship, generosity, and work. This selection has been taken from Aquinas' *Summa Theologiae*, II–II, 66, 2.

♦ ♦ ♦

… private property is necessary for human life for three reasons: First, because each person takes more trouble to care for something that is his sole responsibility than what is held in common or by many—for in such a case each individual shirks the work and leaves the responsibility to somebody else, which is what happens when too many officials are involved. Second, because human affairs are more efficiently organized if each person has his own responsibility to discharge; there would be chaos if everybody cared for everything. Third, because men live together in greater peace where everyone is content with his own (*re sua contentus est*). We do, in fact, notice that quarrels often break out amongst men who hold things in common without distinction.

Carl Menger (1840–1921), in this citation from *Principles of Economics* (1871), highlights the central importance of the notion of property for human interaction. Menger was the founder of the Austrian economic tradition and helped launch the neoclassical economic revolution. Menger recognized, as did many theologians before and after him, the *naturalness* of private ownership—both in terms of the necessity of property for human survival, as well as the result of human personality mingling with the material world.

♦ ♦ ♦

Thus human economy and property have a joint economic origin since both have, as the ultimate reason for their existence, the fact that goods exist whose available quantities are smaller than the requirements of men. Property, therefore, like human economy, is not an arbitrary invention but rather the only practically possible solution of the problem that is, in the nature of things, imposed upon us by the disparity between requirements for, and available quantities of, all economic goods.

As a result, it is impossible to abolish the institution of property without removing the causes that of necessity bring it about—that is, without simultaneously increasing the available quantities of all economic goods to such an extent that the requirements of all members of society can be met completely, or without reducing the needs of men far enough to make the available goods suffice for the complete satisfaction of their needs. Without establishing such an equilibrium between requirements and available amounts, a new social order could indeed ensure that the available quantities of economic goods would be used for the satisfaction of the needs of different persons than at present. But by such a redistribution it could never surmount the fact that there would be persons whose requirements for economic goods would either not be met at all, or met only incompletely, and against whose potential acts of force, the possessors of economic goods would have to be protected. Property, in this sense, is therefore, inseparable from human economy in its social form, and all plans of social reform can be reasonably be directed only toward an appropriate distribution of economic goods but never to the abolition of the institution of property itself.

As the Bishop of Hippo, **Saint Augustine (354–430)** exerted a powerful influence upon all of the culture, theology, and religious development of the Western world. The first excerpt below was taken from a letter addressed to Vincent, a Donatist bishop, whom Augustine exhorts to consider himself desolate in this world in comparison with the world that is to come. No true comfort can come through temporal things. Property may be necessary and natural, but it is not to command our heart's devotion. In the second excerpt, taken from a sermon, Augustine urges his congregation to consider that their failure to share their surplus with the needy is a form of theft. This second selection highlights the universal destination of material goods as complementary to the notion of private ownership.

♦ ♦ ♦

Through love of this true life you ought, then, to consider yourself desolate in this world, no matter what happiness you enjoy. For, just as that is the true life in comparison with which this other, which is so much loved, is not to be called life, however pleasant and prolonged it may be, so that is the true comfort which God promised by the Prophet saying: "I will give them true comfort, peace upon peace" (Isa. 57:18–19). Without this comfort there is more grief than consolation to be found in earthly comforts, whatever they may be. Certainly, as far as riches and high-ranking positions and other things of that sort are concerned—things which mortals think themselves happy to possess, because they have never partaken of that true happiness—what comfort can they bestow, when it is a far better thing not to need them than to excel in them, and when we are tortured by the craving to possess them, but still more by the fear of losing, once we do possess them? Not by such goods do men become good, but having become good otherwise, they make these things good by their good use of them. Therefore, there is no true comfort in these things; rather, it is found where true life is. A man's happiness necessarily must come from the same source as his goodness....

Moreover, the Christian soul understands how much he should avoid stealing another's goods when he realizes that failure to share his surplus with the needy is like to theft. The Lord says: "Give, and it shall be given to you; forgive, and you shall be forgiven" (Luke 6:37–38). Let us graciously and fervently perform these two types of almsgiving, that is, giving and forgiving, for we, in turn, pray the Lord to give us good things and not to requite our evil deeds. "Give, and it shall be given to you," He says. What is truer, what is more just, than that he who refuses to give should cheat himself and not receive? If a farmer is not justified in gathering a harvest when he knows he has sowed no seed, how much more unreasonable for him who has refused to hear the petition of a poor man to expect a generous response from God? For, in the person of the poor, He who experiences no hunger wished Himself to be fed. Therefore, let us not spurn our God who is needy in His poor, so that we in our need may be filled in Him who is rich. We have the needy, and we ourselves have need; let us give, therefore, so that we may receive. In trut what is it that we give? And in return for that pittance which is meagre, visible, temporal, and earthly, what do we desire to receive? What the "eye has not seen nor ear heard, nor has it entered into the heart of man" (1 Cor. 2:4).

Pope Leo XIII (1810–1903) was the father of modern Catholic social teaching. His encyclical *Rerum Novarum* (1891) addressed in systematic fashion the changes and challenges of then-emerging modern society. Attempting to steer the Church between the competing socio-economic systems of socialism and liberalism, Leo condemned socialism while warning against the excesses of liberalism. His condemnation of socialism relied in great part on his affirmation of the right to private property. In the following selection from *Rerum Novarum* (no. 15), the pope defends private ownership as a natural right of the human person.

♦ ♦ ♦

[I]t ... follows that private possessions are clearly in accord with nature. The earth indeed produces in great abundance the things to preserve and, especially, to perfect life, but of itself it could not produce them without human cultivation and care. Moreover, since man expends his mental energy and his bodily strength in procuring the goods of nature, by this very act he appropriates that part of physical nature to himself which he has cultivated. On it he leaves, as it were, a kind of image of his person, so that it must be altogether just that he should possess that part as his very own and that no one in any way should be permitted to violate this right.

Saint John Chrysostom (347–407) may certainly be said to be one of the most brilliant and eloquent exponents of the great themes of Greek patristic social teaching. At the heart of his social thought lies a double principle that sustains and nurtures common life: charity, on the one hand, which is embodied in compassion and sharing; and solidarity, on the other hand, which is expressed in the mutual interdependence of all human beings. These excerpts taken from his homilies illustrate well this double principle. The first two selections emphasize that the bonds of love make the sharing of one's possessions a serious obligation, while the second set expands the notion of stewardship to include "everything wherewith each is entrusted," namely, possessions, riches, food, and time.

♦ ♦ ♦

... For the temporal goods are but an appendage to the spiritual ones, so vile and trifling they are in comparison with these, however great they may be. Let us not therefore spend our energies on them, but regard both the acquisition and the loss of them with equal indifference, like Job who neither clung to them when present, nor sought them absent. On this account riches are called *chremata* (utilities), so that we should not bury them in the earth but should use them aright. Each artisan has his peculiar skill, so does the rich man. The rich man does not know how to work in brass, nor to frame ships, nor to weave, nor to build houses, nor any such thing. Let him then learn to use his wealth aright, and to pity the poor; so will he know a better art than all those.

... This parable (of the faithful servant, Matt. 24:45–47) applies not to money only but also to speech, power, gifts, and every stewardship wherewith each is entrusted. It would suit rulers in the state also, for everyone is bound to make full use of what he has for the common good. If it is wisdom that you have, or power, or wealth, or whatever, let it not be for the ruin of your fellow-servants nor for your own ruin....

Let us who have money listen to these things as well. For Christ speaks not only to teachers but also to the rich. For both have been entrusted with riches: the teachers with the more necessary wealth, the rich with the inferior one. While the teachers are giving out the greater wealth, you are not willing to show forth your generosity even in the lesser, or rather not generosity but honesty (for you are in fact giving things that belong to others), what excuse will you have?

For you too are stewards of your own possessions, no less than he who dispenses the alms of the Church. Just as he has no right to squander at random and at hazard the things given by you for the poor, since they were given for the maintenance of the poor, so you may not squander your own. For even though you have received an inheritance from your father, and have in this way come to possess everything you have, still everything belongs to God.... Therefore though he could have taken these possessions away from you, God left them so that you may have the opportunity to show forth virtue. Thus, bringing us into need one of another, he makes our love for one another more fervent....

Many consider **Adam Smith (1723–1790)** to be the founder of modern economics because he first provided the discipline of economics with several foundational definitions and concepts. The selection below is a defense of the idea that private ownership most effectively employs resources and thus leads to human betterment. It also warns against the inefficiency of the state owning property. As such, it is a brief, but powerful defense of private ownership. This selection was taken from Smith's most well-known work, *An Inquiry into the Nature and Causes of the Wealth of Nations* (1776).

♦ ♦ ♦

What is the species of domestick industry which his capital can employ and of which the produce is likely to be of the greatest value, every individual, it is evident, can, in his local situation, judge much better than any statesman or lawgiver can do for him. The statesman, who should attempt to direct private people in what manner they ought to employ their capitals, would not only load himself with a most unnecessary attention, but assume an authority which could safely be trusted, not only to no single person, but to no council or senate whatever, and which would nowhere be so dangerous as in the hands of a man who had folly and presumption enough to fancy himself fit to exercise it.

TRADE

Trade is a hallmark of economic study as the economy depends upon the exchange of goods and services. Trade can be described as the exchange of goods, services, or ideas between two or more parties. Today, trade is almost exclusively defined in the sale of goods or services for monetary compensation (money). Trade illustrates the concepts of supply and demand and is essential in the study of economics. As economics seeks to explain human choices and behavior, it frequently focuses on trade to exemplify its theories. Adam Smith believed that the desire to trade is an inherent trait among all humans.

Trade originated in ancient times. Food and clothing were the major commodities then, and trade was conducted within local areas, given the limitations on travel. Bartering (the practice of making offers and counter-offers using a variety of trade-worthy materials) was common during this time and is still prevalent in some Third World countries.

As time progressed and the means of travel improved, the volume of trade became more widespread and pronounced. Europeans improved shipping and colonized new lands primarily for the purpose of trading. Indeed, according to Smith, increased trade was a benchmark of a modernizing society.

For trade to occur there must exist a supply of and demand for a certain good. Trade takes place between a producer and a consumer. The producers supply the good to consumers in the hope that the consumers will trade their money for the good. Consumers, on the other hand, must have some desire (demand) to obtain the good as their property. Without the supply-and-demand dichotomy, trade would scarcely take place.

A free-market economy allows for trade to occur with little interference from the government. The term *free* in the phrase "free-market" implies few, if any restrictions on trade. A free-market system assumes that suppliers and consumers will stabilize the economy by acting out of their own self-interest during the trading process (Smith's "invisible hand" theory). For example, as consumers' desires decrease for one product, producers will most likely decrease production of that good. The suppliers' decisions can also affect trade. If one good costs the producers too much to manufacture, they may scale down production (creating scarcity of the product); this would raise the price of the good and induce greater demand among consumers.

In interventionist governments, public institutions often become involved in the trading process. Governments in these situations will try to regulate trade in the name of the public welfare. Interventionists do not believe that trade within a free market will produce benefit for everyone involved; rather, they contend that rules and regulations must be enforced to ensure equity. Examples of interventionist measures include price floors (in which a product's price cannot fall below a government-set limit) and tariffs (limiting the amount of international trade by affixing a high tax on foreign products—an effort to bolster demand for domestic products).

In extreme statist governments, such as Communist regimes, the state controls the means of production for many goods. Trade is therefore extremely limited because the government sets prices and wages and is relatively unresponsive to consumer demand.

John Maynard Keynes (1883–1946) is best-known for his support of government intervention in regulating the perceived destructive tendencies of the business cycle. According to some economists, market activity tends to progress in cycles, or periods of expansion and contraction. Keynes argued that deficit spending and government control of the money supply would ease periods of contraction. Free-market economists strongly disagree with his analysis, arguing that periods of contraction are not always destructive but that government intervention can only make a bad situation worse. The following selection, which was taken from Keynes' classic work *The General Theory of Employment, Interest, and Money* (1936) exhibits his skepticism toward the notions of free trade and free exchange.

♦ ♦ ♦

Thus, the weight of my criticism is directed against the inadequacy of the *theoretical* foundations of the *laissez-faire* doctrine upon which I was brought up and which for many years I taught—against the notion that the rate of interest and the volume of investment are self-adjusting at the optimum level, so that preoccupation with the balance of trade is a waste of time. For we, the faculty of economists, prove to have been guilty of presumptuous error in treating as a puerile obsession what for centuries has been a prime object of practical statecraft.

Under the influence of this faulty theory the City of London gradually devised the most dangerous technique for the maintenance of equilibrium which can possibly be imagined, namely, the technique of bank rate coupled with a rigid parity of the foreign exchanges. For this meant that the objective of maintaining a domestic rate of interest consistent with full employment was wholly ruled out. Since, in practice, it is impossible to neglect the balance of payments, a means of controlling it was evolved which, instead of protecting the domestic rate of interest, sacrificed it to the operation of blind forces.

Regarded as the theory of the individual firm and of the distribution of the product resulting from the employment of a given quantity of resources, the classical theory has made a contribution to economic thinking which cannot be impugned. It is impossible to think clearly on the subject without this theory as a part of one's apparatus of thought. I must not be supposed to question this in calling attention to their neglect of what was valuable in their predecessors. Nevertheless, as a contribution to statecraft, which is concerned with the economic system as a whole and with securing the optimum employment of the system's entire resources, the methods of the early pioneers of economic thinking in the sixteenth and seventeenth centuries may have attained to fragments of practical wisdom which the unrealistic abstractions of Ricardo first forgot and then obliterated. There was wisdom in their intense preoccupation with keeping down the rate of interest by means of usury laws, ... by maintaining the domestic stock of money and by discouraging rises in the wage-unit; and in their readiness in the last resort to restore the stock of money by devaluation, if it had become plainly deficient through an unavoidable foreign drain, a rise in the wage-unit, or any other cause.

Karl Marx (1818–1883) was a German political philosopher and economist who examined a whole array of social issues, including worker alienation and the causes of revolution. In his essay, "The Fetishism of Commodities," he makes the subtle argument that an economy based on trade or free exchange further alienates the worker from the product he produces. As exchanges take place, the object produced is further removed from the original owner—the worker. Marx sees such alienation as an injustice.

♦ ♦ ♦

A commodity is therefore a mysterious thing, simply because in it the social character of men's labor appears to them as an objective character stamped upon the product of that labor; because the relation of the producers to the sum total of their own labor is presented to them as a social relation, existing not between themselves, but between the products of their labor. This is the reason why the products of labor become commodities, social things whose qualities are at the same time perceptible and imperceptible by the senses.... But it is different with commodities. There, the existence between the products of labor which stamps them as commodities, have absolutely no connection with their physical properties and with the material relations arising therefrom. There it is a definite social relation between men, that assumes, in their eyes, the fantastic form of a relation between things. In order, therefore, to find an analogy, we must have recourse to the mist-enveloped regions of the religious world. In that world the productions of the human brain appear as independent being endowed with life and entering into relation both with one another and the human race. So it is in the world of commodities with the products of men's hands. This I call the *fetishism* which attaches itself to the products of labor, so soon as they are produced as commodities, and which is therefore inseparable from the production of commodities.

The fetishism of commodities has its origin, as the foregoing analysis has already shown, in the peculiar social character of the labor that produces them.

As a general rule, articles of utility become commodities only because they are products of the labor of private individual or groups of individuals who carry on their work independently of each other. The sum total of the labor of all these private individuals forms the aggregate labor of society. Since the producers do not come into social contact with each other until they exchange their products, the specific social character of each producer's labor does not show itself except in the act of exchange. In other words, the labor of the individual asserts itself as a part of the labor of society, only by means of the relations which the act of exchange establishes directly between the products, and indirect, therefore, the relations connecting the labor of one individual with that of the rest appear, not as direct social relations between individuals at work, but as what they really are, material relations between persons and social relations between things. It is only by being exchanged that the products of labor acquire, as values, one uniform social status, distinct from their various forms of existence as objects of utility. This division of a product into a useful thing and a value becomes practically important only when exchange has acquired such an extension that useful articles are produced for the purpose of being exchanged, and their character as values has therefore to be taken into account, beforehand, during production.

Free-market economists stand opposed to Marx's understanding of trade as harmful to workers. Economists who understand trade and free exchange as mutually beneficial and thus, good for all, including the worker, argue against socialist interpretations. As such, the economic problems with socialism have been demonstrated often and by many market economists. An early critic of thinkers such as Marx was **Ludwig von Mises (1881–1973).** Von Mises was a student of Carl Menger and a prominent figure in the Austrian school of economics. In his book *Socialism*, Mises explicates the drawbacks that a socialist system brings to the network of free exchange. Such drawbacks limit productivity and thus harm all in society.

♦ ♦ ♦

It is not necessary that each individual should himself consume the whole share allotted to him. He can let some go to waste, give some away, or, as far as the commodity permits, put some aside for later consumption. Some, however, he can exchange. The beer drinker will readily forgo his share of nonalcoholic drink to obtain more beer. The abstainer will be prepared to forgo his claim to spirits if he can acquire other commodities instead. The aesthete will surrender a visit to the cinema for the same of more opportunities to hear good music; the lowbrow will willingly exchange tickets to art galleries for more congenial pleasures. Everyone will be ready to exchange, but the exchange will be confined to consumers' goods. Producers' goods will be *res extra commercium* (things beyond commerce).

Such exchange need not be confined to direct barter: it can also take place indirectly within certain narrow limits. The same reasons which have led to indirect exchange in other types of society will make it advantageous to those exchanging in the socialistic community. It follows that even here there will be opportunity for the use of a general medium of exchange—money.

The role of money in the socialist economy will be fundamentally the same as in a free economic system—that of a general facilitator of exchange. But the significance of this role will be quite different. In a society based on the collective ownership of the means of production, the significance of the role of money will be incomparably narrower than in a society based on private property in the means of production. For in the socialist commonwealth, exchange itself has a much narrower significance, since it is confined to consumers' goods only. There cannot be money prices of producers' goods since these do not enter into exchange. The accounting function which money exercises in production in a free economic order will no longer exist in a socialist community. Money calculations of value will be impossible.

Luis Saravia de la Calle (c.1544) was a Spanish Scholastic from the School of Salamanca. The Spanish School foreshadowed the work of later free-market economists in a remarkable way. The free-market economist Murray Rothbard went so far as to call these theologians the first scientific economists. The following selection, from *Instrucción de Mercaderes*, introduces Saravia's analysis of the origins of prices. He believes that a price of a good or service is ultimately determined in reference to the totality of subjective estimations of worth that occur every day in the economy. This subjective understanding of price proves indispensable for comprehending exchange theory. Subjective valuations of goods and services encourages trade as individuals who possess a good they value less than a good possessed by another will entertain the possibility of trade.

◆ ◆ ◆

Therefore, those who measure the just price by the labour, costs, and risk incurred by the person who deals in the merchandise or produces it, or by the cost of transport, or the expense of travelling to and from the fair, or by what he has to pay the factors for their industry, risk and labour are greatly in error, *and still more so are those who allow a certain profit of a fifth or tenth*. For the just price arises from the abundance or scarcity of goods, merchants and money, as has been said, and not from costs, labour and risk. *If we had to consider labour and risk in order to assess the just price, no merchants would ever suffer a loss, nor would abundance or scarcity of goods and money enter into the question.*

MUTUALLY BENEFICIAL EXCHANGE

When trade occurs, it is most often the case that the parties involved in the exchange both benefit from the transaction. After all, why would either one take part in the exchange if it were not to their advantage? From this fact derives the concept of mutually beneficial exchange.

Mutually beneficial exchange provides the motivating principle for a free economic market. With freedom to trade, people or businesses are able to choose with whom to exchange products and services for money. Both parties are able to express their opinions when looking for trade partners, and both come away having accomplished a certain trade goal. Thus, the exchange is beneficial for both.

Producers are ultimately looking to make a profit in their business. By making products they hope to sell for profit, producers count on the consumers to exercise their freedom of choice and exchange their money for the product. Consumers, meanwhile, demand certain products and are willing to trade their money to obtain the satisfaction of acquiring such products. At the end of the exchange, both are better off than they were before.

Mutually beneficial exchange is sometimes deterred in systems that do not practice free-market economics. In statist and interventionist governments, freedom to choose among consumers and producers is severely hindered. Choices are limited, as are incentives for producers to create competitive products.

The notion of mutually beneficial exchange is ironic; it benefits all involved, while the primary goal of each individual party is to benefit only himself.

Congregationalist minister **Edmund A. Opitz (1914–)** considers *Religion and Capitalism: Allies, Not Enemies* (1970). Opitz contends in this excerpt that free exchange is one of the aspects of the free market that serves the common good most powerfully and that improper state interference in exchange damages its beneficial quality.

♦ ♦ ♦

Man is the kind of creature who seeks to economize scarce goods, and so he invents labor-saving devices. The primordial labor-saving device is the market, which enables men to freely exchange the results of their specialization for items they prefer. In a typical economic transaction you walk into a bookstore and stumble upon a volume which you need to complete a set; it is in good condition and the price of two dollars is right, so you buy it. You are delighted to exchange your two dollars for the book, and the proprietor who had been anxious to sell it is happy to have your money. Satisfactions on both sides of this exchange have been enhanced.

But there are other kinds of action in society where goods and services are not exchanged for goods and services to the benefit of both parties; there is theft, and predation, and violence. The same human drives which issue in economic action; namely, the need to economize on scarce means, might drive a man into theft for, as has been observed, robbery is a labor-saving device. There is only one way by which wealth comes into being, and that is by production; but there are two ways by which wealth may be acquired: first, by producing it, and secondly, by helping yourself to the fruits of someone else's production.

Contingencies of this sort in society create a demand for the protection of the peaceful and productive activities of men, that is to say, for government. The market is simply a name for the peaceful and voluntary exchange of goods and services occurring constantly between people who trade the results of their specializations. It is the organization of peaceful means. Policing, by contrast, is the regulated use of force against peacebreakers for the protection of peaceful people; it is the organization of coercive means. When a policeman overtakes a thief and forces him to disgorge the items he has stolen, he may use something stronger than persuasion; he may use a club or a gun. In any event, the policing transaction, in contrast to the economic exchange, does not enhance the general level of well-being of both parties to the exchange. Policing, in other words, cannot be organized as a market transaction; although policing costs money it is not within the domain of economics.

Michael Novak (1933–) is one of the foremost contemporary Christian thinkers seeking to offer a synthesis between the free-market system and the Christian faith. In this piece from perhaps his most seminal work, *The Catholic Ethic and the Spirit of Capitalism,* Novak extols the virtues of free exchange and counters the argument that liberty entails disorder. Novak's defense of liberty undergirds his defense of mutually beneficial exchanges, which, by their nature, must be freely entered into.

◆ ◆ ◆

[Traditionalists] tend to imagine that liberty *must* lead to chaos. Where there is liberty, they think, each person will go off in a different direction, at whim, or in pursuit of crass self-interest without order. Only the law, they imagine, or only a strong leader (a *caudillo*) can hold other wills in check, channel them—and make the trains run on time.

In traditional cultures, this may be so. But in cultures based upon free and dynamic markets, purely *centrifugal* activities would be self-defeating. For there is one secret to the free society that traditionalists do not grasp: The free market is a *centripetal* force. Where it is truly dynamic, based upon invention and innovation, and where it is animated by a culture that believes in fair play and obeying the rules, the free market obliges those who would succeed in it to pay attention to others—even to the unexpressed wants and desires of others; even to their right to basic respect and dignity. For they are obliged to approach others only through the latter's freely given consent....

Thus the insight most lacking to traditionalists is that intelligent and practical persons, acting freely and on behalf of their own practical wisdom, can in their free exchanges generate a spontaneous order, a form of catallaxy superior in its reasonableness to any order that might be planned, directed, or enforced from above. Traditionalists seem to believe that the only possible order is order enforced from on high. Order, in the traditionalist view, is first an intellectual construct conceived in the mind of the leader, then promulgated, then enforced. In a free society the concept of order is quite different. When free persons try to be cooperative, and attempt to enter into reasonable contracts with their fellows, these very efforts give rise to a social order more alive with intelligence, and more subtly and gracefully ordered, than all the planned and top-down orders on earth.

That free markets, under certain cultural and political conditions, will produce a superior social order should be treated as an empirical hypothesis. Such a statement would be true only if, under extended social experiments, the predicted consequences did in fact occur. The prediction of the *traditionalists* is that a free society will lack all order. The prediction of those who believe in the power of *free markets* to encourage reasonable and cooperative behavior is that such markets will give rise to a more dynamic order, shot through with greater intelligence and a wider and deeper intelligibility, than any known alternative. Try out these two hypotheses and see for yourself.

George Gilder (1939–) highlights the benefits of free trade and the misconceptions of those who fret over trade imbalances. In this selection from *Recapturing the Spirit of Enterprise* (1992), Gilder recounts the history of United States trade to show that free exchange is generally a beneficial phenomenon.

◆ ◆ ◆

The reason that most economists cannot comprehend the 1980s is that it was a period of entrepreneurial acceleration. While economists measured the deficit and the trade gap, entrepreneurs were multiplying value at an unprecedented pace and disguising it with plummeting prices.

The second great error of the critics of U.S. competitiveness is their focus on trade gap figures. They assume that a trade surplus is a signal of competitive superiority and a trade gap is a sign of weakness. But many of the slowest-growing economies in the world, from Argentina to Tanzania, run trade surpluses. A sluggish economy cannot generate the wealth to import more than it exports.

By the rules of accounting, a trade surplus signifies capital flight or a relative decline in domestic investment opportunities; a trade gap suggests a capital surplus caused by a flow of investments to the economy with the trade deficit. While the U.S. trade deficit exploded in the early and mid-1980s, the United States was the world's fastest-growing major industrial economy, and the dollar surged in value, signifying that the trade gap was caused by an inflow of capital rather than by a shortfall of competitiveness.

The United States almost always ran trade deficits during its most prosperous periods and surpluses during the Depression. During the first two decades after World War II, Japan ran a trade deficit every year and was the world's fastest-growing economy for most of that period. During the 1970s and 1980s, Korea and other Asian countries replaced Japan as global growth champions; Korea ran a trade deficit until 1985. Korea was regarded as a dangerous debtor by the many economists who did not understand the dynamics of trade and money in an integrated world economy.

One way to look at the trade deficit of the early and mid-1980s, when the United States was the fastest-growing major economy, is to say that U.S. businesses were the world's only exporters who lacked the privilege of exporting to the booming U.S. market. Leading the U.S. domestic expansion was the computer industry. Therefore, the importing of foreign-made computer components accounted for an ever-rising share of the U.S. trade deficit. Statisticians mistakenly interpreted this gap as suggesting a decline in U.S. competitiveness in computers. On the contrary, the trade gap of the 1980s, particularly in computer components, suggested the rising competitiveness of the United States. It was the decline in the trade deficit in the early 1990s that signified a portentous decline in the entrepreneurial vitality of the U.S. economy.

With global capital markets on line twenty-four hours a day and goods markets hobbled by protectionism and politics, flows of capital are now more significant than flows of goods in determining a balance of trade. Most economists suffer from the outdated notion of significant distinction between assets (for example, land, hotels, technologies, or corporate equities) and products (computers, chips, capital equipment, films, software packages, sides of beef, oranges). But in the current world economy, assets have become as reproduceable and tradable as other products or services. The chief difference is that when the Japanese buy an orange or side of beef, they eat it and we do not have it anymore; but after they buy hotels in the United States or American technology licenses, we still have them, along with new funds to direct toward the creation of yet more valuable assets in the future. That is why all during the mid-1980s when the Japanese were splurging on our assets, the total value of American assets was growing at an unprecedented pace and the average U.S. citizen approximately tripled his asset holdings.

The critics of U.S. competitiveness interpret these developments as a menace to the future of the U.S. economy, which they claim will be laden with debts to foreigners. Apparently unconscious of the globalization of capital markets, the critics seem to suppose that dollars accruing to a foreign firm are less likely to be reinvested in the United States than the dollars of an American firm. But in either case, the capital will flow toward the best foreign equities as well as does Ako Morita of Sony. In recent years, Honda has invested a larger portion of its profiles in the investment climate by barring outsiders, both Americans and foreigners will send their investments elsewhere. If the United States favors entrepreneurship and creativity, both Americans and foreigners will continue to send money and talent here and we will continue to run a trade deficit in the less important categories, the ones stressed by the economists.

VALUE AND PRICE THEORIES

Fundamental to economic theory is price and value theory. Economic value implies the actual worth of a particular good or service while price denotes the actual market expression of that worth in terms of currency. The key to understanding both value and price theory is subjective value. By subjective value, economists explain that goods and services have no intrinsic economic value in themselves, but only the value that a potential consumer or producer imputes to the good or service in question. For example, how much is a pair of shoes worth? There is no real answer to this question; rather, the answer is dependent on the estimations of producers and consumers in the market at any given time. To assert that economic value is subjective is not to assert that other values, such as moral values, are subjective.

Price theory is often used to describe the way people seek to maximize their utility (satisfaction with the trade) given the prices available to them. Price theory is concerned with how much the producers have to spend in order to create and sell the good and how consumers can rationally pay for the product in order to achieve satisfaction. The suppliers' costs might include: materials to make the product; the rent on a facility where the goods are produced; and wages paid to workers who build the product. Every expense that goes into the production of the good per one unit of the good can be considered. When this number is calculated, a price is affixed to the good for sale to consumers. Frequently, this figure is set so that the costs to make and sell the product are covered, as well as some amount of profit (taking in more than your costs). At the same time, consumers are deciding how to purchase products they want or need with the prices with which they are faced. Using price theory often assumes that the suppliers and the customers will act rationally in order to achieve their trade goals efficiently.

Value theory is not as strongly associated with fixed numbers as is price theory. In value theory, it is assumed that a product is worth only as much as the consumer values having that product. In other words, the consumer's attitude toward the good is what really determines its worth and ultimately its price. For example, a person who lives in Florida probably has very little use for a snow blower. Regardless of how much the machine costs to produce, this person will have little interest in acquiring it and thus will assign a small value to it (meaning he is willing to pay only a low price for the machine). However, a person living in Minnesota may value that same machine much more and may be willing to pay even more than the producer's suggested price to obtain the machine. The value, then, is more closely associated with attitudes toward products rather than attitudes toward prices.

It is important to note that neither producers nor consumers alone determine the natural prices of goods. Both the supply of the producers and the demand of the consumers must exist for prices to be set. Value and price theories seek to provide explanations for changes or shifts in the supply or demand cycles.

Value and price theories attempt to clarify from different angles how worth is assigned to products. The theories provide further insight into the dynamic relationship of trade among producers and consumers.

In this passage from his *Principles of Economics* (1871), **Carl Menger** explicates the subjective nature of economic values.

♦ ♦ ♦

The value, that is the exchange value, of one thing in terms of another at any place and time, is the amount of that second thing which can be got there and then in exchange for the first. Thus the term *value* is relative, and expresses the relation between two things at a particular place and time.

Civilized countries generally adopt gold or silver or both as money. Instead of expressing the values of lead and tin, and wood, and corn and other things in terms of one another, we express them in terms of money in the first instance; and call the value of each thing thus expressed its *price*. If we know that a ton of lead will exchange for fifteen sovereigns at any place and time, while a ton of tin will exchange for ninety sovereigns, we say that their prices then and there are £15 and £90 respectively, and we know that the value of a ton of tin in terms of lead is six tons then and there....

The price of every thing rises and falls from time to time and place to place; and with every such change the purchasing power of money changes as far as that thing goes. If the purchasing power of money rises with regard to some things, and at the same time falls equally with regard to equally important things, its general purchasing power (or its power of purchasing things in general) has remained stationary. This phrase conceals some difficulties, which we must study later on. But meanwhile we may take it in its popular sense, which is sufficiently clear; and we may throughout this volume neglect possible changes in the general purchasing power of money. Thus the price of anything will be taken as representative of its exchange value relative to things in general, or in other words as representative of its general purchasing power.

For **Luis de Molina (1535–1600)**, a just price is based on a subjective theory of value. Molina, a member of the Salamanca School, argues that a just price for a given good is whatever price the market will assign to an item—with the price having been voluntarily agreed upon by the relevant parties. The following selection is from Molina's *La Teoria del Justo Prico*.

♦ ♦ ♦

In the first place, it should be observed that a price is considered just or unjust not because of the nature of the things themselves—this would lead us to value them according to their nobility or perfection—but due to their ability to serve human utility. Because this is the way in which they are appreciated by men, they therefore command a price in the market and in exchanges. Moreover, this is the end for which God gave things to man, and with that same end men divided among them the domain of all things, even though they belonged to everybody at the moment of their creation. What we have just described explains why rats, which, according to their nature, are nobler than wheat, are not esteemed or appreciated by men. The reason is that they are of no utility whatsoever. This also explains why a house can be justly sold at a higher price than a horse and even a slave, even though the horse and the slave are, by nature, much nobler than the house.

In the second place, we should observe that the just price of goods is not fixed according to the utility given to them by man, as if, *ceteris paribus*, the nature and the need of the use given to them determined the quantity of price … it *depends on the relative appreciation which each man has for the use of the good.* This explains why the just price of a pearl, which can be used only to decorate, is higher than the just price of a great quantity of grain, wine, meat, bread, or horses, even if the utility of these things (which are also nobler in nature) is more convenient and superior to the use of a pearl. That is why *we can conclude that the just price for a pearl depends on the fact that some men wanted to grant it value* as an object of decoration.

Like the earlier selection from **John Maynard Keynes**, this call for consistency between value theory and price theory comes from his *General Theory of Employment, Interest, and Money* (1936).

♦ ♦ ♦

So long as economists are concerned with what is called the Theory of Value, they have been accustomed to teach that prices are governed by the conditions of supply and demand; and, in particular, changes in marginal cost and the elasticity of short-period supply have played a prominent part. But when they pass in volume II, or more often in a separate treatise, to the Theory of Money and Prices, we hear no more of these homely but intelligible concepts and move into a world where prices are governed by the quantity of money, by its income-velocity, by the velocity of circulation relative to the volume of transactions, by hoarding, by forced saving, by inflation and deflation *et hoc genus omne*; and little or no attempt is made to relate these vaguer phrases to our former notions of the elasticities of supply and demand. If we reflect on what we are being taught and try to rationalise it, in the simpler discussions it seems that the elasticity of supply must have become zero and demand proportional to the quantity of money; whilst in the more sophisticated we are lost in a haze where nothing is clear and everything is possible. We have all of us become used to finding ourselves some times on the one side of the moon and sometimes on the other, without knowing what route or journey connects them, related, apparently, after the fashion of our waking and our dreaming lives.

One of the objects of the foregoing chapters has been to escape from this double life and to bring the theory of prices as a whole back to close contact with the theory of value. The division of Economics between the Theory of Value and Distribution on the one hand and the Theory of Money on the other hand is, I think, a false division. The right dichotomy is, I suggest, between the Theory of the Individual Industry or Firm and of the rewards and the distribution between different uses of a *given* quantity of resources on the one hand, and the Theory of Output and

Employment *as a whole* on the other hand. So long as we limit ourselves to the study of the individual industry or firm on the assumption that the aggregate quantity of employed resources is constant, and, provisionally, that the conditions of other industries or firms are unchanged, it is true that we are not concerned with the significant characteristics of money. But as soon as we pass to the problem of what determines output and employment as a whole, we require the complete theory of a Monetary Economy.

E. F. Schumacher (1911–1977), in this passage from *Small Is Beautiful* (1945), explains why theories such as those having to do with price and value are necessarily limited. He makes it clear that admitting the economically subjective value of a given item does not diminish the objective value (ontological value) it might have as a part of creation. By making this distinction, Schumacher further elaborates the subjective nature of economic value.

◆ ◆ ◆

It is hardly an exaggeration to say that, with increasing affluence, economics has moved into the very centre of public concern, and economic performance, economic growth, economic expansion, and so forth have become the abiding interest, if not the obsession, of all modern societies. In the current vocabulary of condemnation there are few words as final and conclusive as the word "uneconomic." If an activity has been branded as uneconomic, its right to existence is not merely questioned but energetically denied. Anything that is found to be an impediment to economic growth is a shameful thing, and if people cling to it, they are thought of as either saboteurs or fools. Call a thing immoral or ugly, soul-destroying or a degradation of man, a peril to the peace of the world or to the well-being of future generations; as long as you have not shown it to be "uneconomic" you have not really questioned its right to exist, grow, and prosper....

Something is uneconomic when it fails to earn an adequate profit in terms of money. The method of economics does not, and cannot, produce any other meaning. Numerous attempts have been made to obscure this fact, and they have caused a very great deal of confusion; but the fact remains. Society, or a group or an individual within society, may decide to hang on to an activity or asset *for noneconomic reasons*—social, aesthetic, moral, or political—but this does in no way alter its *uneconomic* character. The judgment of economics, in other words, is an extremely *fragmentary judgment*; out of the large number of aspects which in real life have to be seen and judged together before a decision can be taken, economics supplies only one—whether a thing yields a money profit *to those who undertake it* or not.

However that may be, about the *fragmentary* nature of the judgments of economics there can be no doubt whatever. Even within the narrow compass of the economic calculus, these judgments are necessarily and *methodically* narrow. For one thing, they give vastly more weight to the short than to the long-term, because in the long-term, as Keynes put it with cheerful brutality, we are all dead.

Economics, moreover, deals with goods in accordance with their market value and does not in accordance with what they really are. The same rules and criteria are applied to primary goods, which man has to win from nature, and secondary goods, which presuppose the existence of primary goods and are manufactured from them. All goods are treated the same, because the point of view is fundamentally that of private profit-making, and this means that it is inherent in the methodology of economics *to ignore man's dependence on the natural world.*

In the marketplace, for practical reasons, unnumerable qualitative distinctions which are of vital importance for man and society are suppressed; they are not allowed to surface. Thus the reign of quantity celebrates its greatest triumphs in "The Market." Everything is equated with everything else. To equate things means to give them a price and thus to make the exchangeable. To the extent that economic thinking is based on the market, it takes the sacredness out of life, because there can be nothing sacred in something that has a price. Not surprisingly, therefore is economic thinking pervades the whole of society, even simple noneconomic values like beauty, health, or cleanliness can survive only if they prove to be "economic."

David Ricardo (1772–1823) was an English economist who challenged the notion of subjective value theory. Ricardo argues in this excerpt from *On the Principles of Political Economy and Taxation* (1811) that labor ought to be the determinant of value. The labor theory of value later provided Marx and other socialist thinkers with an opportunity to criticize Ricardo's understanding of capitalism. If Ricardo had accepted the subjective theory of value, Marx and his collaborators would have had more difficulty in making a case against free markets.

◆ ◆ ◆

It has been observed by Adam Smith, that "the word Value has two different meanings, and sometimes expresses the utility of some particular object, and sometimes the power of purchasing other goods which the possession of that object conveys. The one may be called *value in use*; the other *value in exchange*. The things," he continues, "which have the greatest value in use, have frequently little or no value in exchange; and, on the contrary, those which have the greatest value in exchange, have little or no value in use." Water and air are abundantly useful; they are indeed indispensable to existence, yet, under ordinary circumstances, nothing can be obtained in exchange for them. Gold, on the contrary, though of little use compared with air or water, will exchange for a great quantity of other goods.

Utility then is not the measure of exchangeable value, although it is absolutely essential to it. If a commodity were in no way useful—in other words, if it could in no way contribute to our gratification—it would be destitute of exchangeable value, however scarce it might be, or whatever quantity of labour might be necessary to procure it.

Possessing utility, commodities derive their exchangeable value from two sources: from their scarcity, and from the quantity of labour required to obtain them.

There are some commodities, the value of which is determined by their scarcity alone. No labour can increase the quantity of such goods, and therefore their value cannot be lowered by an increased supply. Some rare statues and pictures, scarce books and coins, wines of a peculiar quality, which can be made only from grapes grown on a particular soil, of which there is a very limited quantity, are all of this description. Their value is wholly independent of the quantity of labour originally necessary to produce them, and varies with the varying wealth and inclinations of those who are desirous to possess them.

These commodities, however, form a very small part of the mass of commodities daily exchanged in the market. By far the greatest part of those goods which are the objects of desire, are procured by labour; and they may be multiplied, not in one country alone, but in many almost without any assignable limit, if we are disposed to bestow the labour necessary to obtain them.

One of **Karl Marx's** principal contentions involves the surplus theory of value, sometimes referred to as the *labor theory of value*. Marx, following

Ricardo, realized that given the current classical scheme of value and price, the profit of an item could be attributed to the value of the labor added in production. This, therefore, appeared to indicate that employers and owners who benefited from profits were "living off the backs of the workers." Marx's theory of value, and the subsequent moral dilemma, were rendered moot when Carl Menger published his *Principles of Economics* (1871). The following selection was taken from Marx's *Capital: A Critique of Political Economy* (1867).

◆ ◆ ◆

Capital has not invented surplus labour. Wherever a part of society possesses the monopoly of the means of production, the labourer free or not free must add to the working time necessary for his own maintenance an extra working time in order to produce the means of subsistence for the owners of the means of production, whether this proprietor be the Athenian *kalos kagatnos*, Etruscan theocrat, *civis Romanus*, Norman baron, American slave owner, Wallachian Boyard, modern landlord, or capitalist. It is, however, clear that in any given economic formation of society, where not the exchange value but the use-value of the product predominates, surplus labour will be limited by a given set of wants which may be greater or less, and that here no boundless thirst for surplus labour arises from the nature of the production itself. Hence in antiquity, overwork becomes horrible only when the object is to obtain exchange value in its specific independent money form, in the production of gold and silver. Compulsory working to death is here the recognized form of overwork. Only read Diodorus Siculus. Still these are exceptions in antiquity. But as soon as people, whose production still moves within the lower forms of slave labour, corvee labour, and the like, are drawn into the whirlpool of an international market dominated by the capitalistic mode of production, the sale of their products for export becoming their principal interest, the civilised horrors of overwork are grafted on the barbaric horrors of slavery and serfdom. Hence the Negro labour in the Southern States of the American Union preserved something of a patriarchal character so long as production was chiefly directed to immediate local consumption. But in proportion, as the export of cotton became of vital interest to these states, the overworking of the Negro and sometimes the using up of his life in seven years of labour became a factor in a calculated and calculating system. It was no longer a question of obtaining from him a certain quantity of useful products. It was now a question of production of surplus labour itself.

The Austrian school of economics later offered this corrective to the labor theory of value proposed by Ricardo. **Thomas C. Taylor (1928–)**, associate of the Ludwig von Mises Institute, explains the Austrian view of subjective value in this selection from *An Introduction to Austrian Economics* (1980).

◆ ◆ ◆

The explanation of all economic activity that takes place in the market economy ultimately rests on the subjective theory of value. The value of various consumer goods and services does not reside objectively and intrinsically in the things themselves, apart from the individual who is making an evaluation. His valuation is a subjective matter that even he cannot reduce to objective terms or measurement. Valuation consists in preferring a particular increment of a thing over increments of alternative things available; the outcome of valuation is the ranking of definite quantities of various goods and services with which the individual is concerned for purposes of decision and action. Theory resorts to the hypothetical concept of the scale of values in seeking to explain and understand the nature of human valuations. The ranking of alternative ends is determined by the person's expectations of satisfaction from each other specific choice faced by him at any moment of decision. He will invariably select the alternative that he believes will yield him the greatest satisfaction.

The subjectiveness of valuation rests in the nature of satisfaction—satisfaction is subjective and not open to numerical measurement. The extent to which a thing gives satisfaction is always personal. People derive satisfaction from different goods and services; that is, all people are not alike in terms of the types of things that please them. Experience also demonstrates that a person's preferences vary from time to time. His ranking of alternative choices may undergo a reshuffling at any given moment. His scale of values may also be altered by deletions or additions.

To relate the matter of valuation to the individual person is not to suggest that each individual is concerned only with the satisfaction of his own appetites and needs. A person may find satisfaction or relief in helping another person. Satisfaction can be and often is derived from the attainment of altruistic as well as "selfish" motives. But the point remains that regardless of the form the satisfaction is to take, each choice arises from subjective valuation on the part of the particular person who is doing the choosing. The uneasiness that he seeks to remove is in his own mind, whether such uneasiness pertains to an immediate problem of his own or to a problem faced by someone else. His choice stems from the preference that he has for the removal of a particular uneasiness over another problem to which he could devote his attention.

A student of Ludwig von Mises, **Israel Kirzner (1932–)**, is professor of economics at New York University. In his seminal text, *Perception, Opportunity, and Profit* (1986), he makes the case for the inherent justice of market prices.

♦ ♦ ♦

No examination of the possibility of injustice in market transfers can avoid some reference to recent discussions of the medieval doctrines of just price. Earlier scholars understood the medieval writers to have seen *cost of production* as the criterion for justice in pricing. An unjust price for a good was one that diverged from its true value as defined by production costs, with the later "determined by a fixed standard of living on the part of the producers and ... not to include any element of *interest*." An unjust price was thus seen as unjust not primarily because it involved deceit by the one party (or at least an error on the part of the second), but simply because justice requires that each party to an exchange receive the true value of what he has given up. If divergence from the true value is described as involving "cheating," this must then mean either merely that without deceit it would presumably be impossible to secure more than the true value of what one gives up, or that to cheat is to be *defined* purely in terms of divergence from true value. (Compare the phrase Nozick used in describing the old question about the possibility of profits: How can there be profits if everything gets its full value, if no *cheating* goes on?") For decades after 1870, economists found it necessary to explain how inadequate such a conception of justice in transfer, ignoring all demand considerations, must be considered. And in Nozick's entitlement theory little room seems to be assigned for divergence from production costs as a criterion for injustice in transfer. (In referring to the possibility of "gouging," Nozick seems quite content to leave to buyers the responsibility of looking out for themselves.

More recently, however, historians of medieval economic thought have emphasized references in the Scholastic writings to market price as the criterion for justice. And such references are occasionally couched in language suggesting that to take advantage of imperfect knowledge of market conditions on the part of one's trading partner is to violate the canons of the just price. But it appears to be incorrect to ascribe to the medieval writers the concern for the possible injustice of disequilibrium market transfers I have expressed here. Whether, with Schumpeter and De Roover, one is prepared to credit Aquinas and the medieval writers with a sophisticated understanding of the relationship between cost of production and long-run equilibrium price, or whether, with Hollander, one is not prepared to do so, it seems fairly clear that for Aquinas actual market price is understood as being always the equilibrium price. It was because the market price was therefore seen as expressing the true value of a good, reflecting "the entire set of objective and subjective elements which forms the community estimate," that it was considered unjust to take advantage of a buyer's ignorance of the market price. It is true that pure profits were, as Hollander has explained, generally frowned upon by Aquinas, but this was clearly on grounds other than the taking advantage of the ignorance of one's trading partners. In other contexts it was clearly not considered unjust to take advantage of another's ignorance. A number of writers have drawn attention to Aquinas's view that a seller may charge a high price for grain in a place where it is dear, even though he knows that others are following with more supplies—a fact that, if known to the buyers, would have led them to refuse to pay the present higher price. Clearly a price paid out of ignorance of the true facts does not, in this view, by itself mark it as unjust.

Aquinas's justification for this permissive position clearly implies that the market price at a given instant is the true equilibrium price relevant to questions of justice. The present high value of the grain is its true present value. The anticipated arrival of additional supplies of grain can be expected to lower the market price *in the future*, so that a seller who sells at today's price does not act unjustly in failing to disclose what will happen in the future. One can understand that if the market price is considered the just price because it reflects the current "community estimate" of value, then information concerning the future possessed by a single market participant may not be seen as altering the present community estimate; and his exploitation of his superior information need not, therefore, be seen as unjust according to the criterion adopted. But if one questions the justice of market exchange precisely because it occurs under conditions one of the parties is ignorant about (so that his consent to the deal might be said to hinge on a wholly erroneous perception of the relevant circumstances) then the Scholastic insight into the justice of market price has not helped us answer our question. Our awareness that market prices are never equilibrium prices does not encourage us to accept the market prices as just because they are somehow expressive of *all* relevant circumstances. These prices, we must recognize, necessarily reflect the very errors that have occasioned our concern.

Juan de Lugo (1583–1660) another Late-Spanish Scholastic from the School at Salamanca builds upon the insight of Molina concerning the subjective nature of economic value. In the following selection Lugo observes that the fluctuation in price of a given commodity can be explained, in part, by variances in valuation on the part of individual consumers.

◆ ◆ ◆

Price fluctuates not because of the intrinsic and substantial perfection of the articles—since mice are more perfect than corn and yet are worth less—but on account of their utility in respect of human need, and then only on account of estimation; for jewels are much less useful than corn in the house, and yet their price is much higher. And we must take into account not only the estimation of prudent men but also of the imprudent, if they are sufficiently numerous in a place. This is why our glass trinkets in Ethiopia justly exchanged for gold, because they are more commonly esteemed there. And among the Japanese old objects made of iron and pottery, which are worth nothing to us, fetch a high price because of their antiquity. Communal estimation, even when foolish, raises the natural price of goods, since price is derived from estimation. The natural price is raised by abundance of buyers and money, and lowered by the contrary factors.

INTERVENTION

Intervention may be described as an interference with natural market processes. Natural market processes are understood as the free exchanges engaged in by individuals throughout the economy. Intervention therefore limits trade. In most cases, intervention involves a governmental attempt to influence trade between two or more parties.

In antiquity, merchants and city-states openly traded with each other, often using the bartering method. With the fall of the Roman Empire and the rise of medieval kingdoms, rulers extended their authority through inter-kingdom trading, but village merchants were by-and-large allowed to trade their products as they pleased.

Intervention in trade gained proponents during the latter part of the Industrial Revolution, when large corporations and businesses began reaping huge profits. In the United States, particularly, where the perceived "robber-barons" came to dominate the market, many interventionist laws were adopted. These have taken many forms: tariffs, price floors and ceilings, anti-monopoly measures, anti-cartel measures, luxury and excise taxes, and production limits.

Intervention ultimately rests on the notion that the market cannot properly regulate itself. Interventionists argue that governmental involvement is necessary so that certain actors in the supply and demand dichotomy are not placed at an "unfair" disadvantage. For example, to benefit consumers of rental housing, government may set a price ceiling on apartment rents, meaning that rent cannot go above a certain price. This measure is designed to help those less affluent gain housing by assuring that rents do not skyrocket. On the downside, however, a shortage of housing usually occurs from price ceilings, as developers cannot effectively supply the number of units demanded by the public.

Suppliers may also receive some benefit from intervention; in these cases the consumers feel the negative effects. In the event of international

101

trade embargoes, domestic suppliers' products become the only options for consumers. This can result in scarcity, which produces higher prices for the consumer.

Many so-called "free-market" systems are not devoid of some form of interventionist policies. Some policies are political in nature, such as isolationist governments forbidding foreign trade, and some are concerned with economic equality (preventing outrageous prices for basic products).

Governments practicing intervention usually believe that they are employing such measures for the benefit of society. In most cases, however, it has been shown that someone is placed at a disadvantage by the state's policies. Debates over the extent of the federal government's involvement with the marketplace continue to rage in the United States and elsewhere.

Milton Friedman (1912–) won the Nobel prize for economics in 1976. The following passage is from *Free to Choose* (1979), co-authored with his wife Rose. The Friedmans here underline the ways in which economic freedom is compromised, often subtly, by the interventions of government.

♦ ♦ ♦

An essential part of economic freedom is freedom to choose how to use our income: how much to spend on ourselves and on what items; how much to save and in what form; how much to give away and to whom. Currently, more than 40 percent of our income is disposed of on our behalf by government at federal, state, and local levels combined. One of us once suggested a new national holiday, "Personal Independence Day— that day in the year when we stop working to pay the expenses of government ... and start working to pay for the items we severally and individually choose in light of our own needs and desires." In 1929 that holiday would have come on Abraham Lincoln's birthday, February 12; today it would come about May 30; if present trends were to continue, it would coincide with the other Independence Day, July 4, around 1988.

Of course, we have something to say about how much of our income is spent on our behalf by government. We participate in the political process that has resulted in government's spending an amount equal to more than 40 percent of our income. Majority rule is a necessary and desirable expedient. It is, however, very different from the kind of freedom you have when you shop at a supermarket. When you enter the voting booth once a year, you almost always vote for a package rather than for specific items. If you are in the majority, you will at best get both the items you favored and the ones you opposed but regarded as on balance less important. Generally, you end up with something different from what you thought you voted for. If you are in the minority, you must conform to the majority vote and wait for your turn to come. When you vote daily in the supermarket, you get precisely what you voted for, and so does everyone else. The ballot box produces conformity without unanimity; the marketplace, unanimity without conformity. That is why it is desirable to use the ballot box, so far as possible, only for those decisions where conformity is essential....

Another essential part of economic freedom is freedom to use the resources we possess in accordance with our own values—freedom to enter any occupation, engage in any business enterprise, buy from and sell to anyone else, so long as we do so on a strictly voluntary basis and do not resort to force in order to coerce others.

Today you are not free to offer your services as a lawyer, a physician, a dentist, a plumber, a barber, a mortician, or engage in a host of other occupations without first getting a permit or license from a government official. You are not free to work overtime at terms mutually agreeable to you and your employer, unless the terms conform to rules and regulations laid down by a government official.

You are not free to set up a bank, go into the taxicab business, or the business of selling electricity or telephone service, or running a railroad, busline, or airline, without first receiving permission from a government official....

It would take a book much longer than this one to list in full all the restrictions on our economic freedom, let alone describe them in detail. These examples are intended simply to suggest how pervasive such restrictions have become.

"Economic Justice for All" is the title of a pastoral letter issued by the **Roman Catholic Bishops of the United States** in 1986. The pastoral letter was issued to call attention to concerns for economic justice in American society. In this passage, the American hierarchy insists that government respect the sovereignty of other spheres of economic activity, including family and local organizations. This is an example of the application of the principle of subsidiarity, a theme from Christian social teaching that calls for limited intervention in the market by government.

♦ ♦ ♦

First, in an advanced industrial economy like ours, all parts of society, including government, must cooperate in forming national economic policies. Taxation, monetary policy, high levels of government spending, and many other forms of governmental regulation are here to stay. A modern economy without governmental interventions of the sort we have alluded to is inconceivable. These interventions, however, should help, not replace, the contributions of other economic actors and institutions and should direct them to the common good. The development of effective new forms of partnership between private and public agencies will be difficult in a situation as immensely complex as that of the United States in which various aspects of national policy seem to contradict one another.... On the theoretical level, achieving greater coordination will make demands on these with the technical competence to analyze the relationship among different parts of the economy. More practically, it will require the various subgroups within our society to sharpen their concern for the common good and moderate their efforts to protect their own short-term interests.

Ludwig von Mises wrote *A Critique of Interventionism* in 1929. It represents a philosophical defense of individual autonomy against the coercion of government force. Mises groups together Marxists and democratic statists as operating within the same interventionist paradigm.

♦ ♦ ♦

Interventionism seeks to retain private property in the means of production, but authoritative commands, especially prohibitions, are to restrict the actions of private owners. If this restriction reaches the point that all important decisions are made along lines of authoritative command, if it is no longer the profit motive of landowners, capitalists, and entrepreneurs, but reasons of state, that decide what is to be produced and how it is produced, then we have socialism even if we retain the private property label.... Public ownership in the means of production is nothing but socialism or communism.

However, interventionism does not want to go that far. It does not seek to abolish private property in production; it merely wants to limit it. On the one hand, it considers unlimited private property harmful to society, and on the other hand, it deems the public property order unrealizable completely, at least for the present. Therefore, it seeks to create a third order: a social system that occupies the center between the private property order and the public property order. Thus, it seeks to avoid the "excesses" and evils of capitalism, but to retain the advantages of individual initiative and industry which socialism cannot bring forth.

The champions of this private property order, which is guided, regulated, and controlled by the state and other social organizations, are making demands that have always been made by political leaders and masses of people. When economics was yet unknown, and man was unaware that good prices cannot be "set" arbitrarily but are narrowly determined by the market situation, government commands sought to regulate economic life. Only classical economics revealed that all such interventions in the functioning of the market can never achieve the objectives which the authorities aim to achieve. The old liberalism which built its economic policies on the teachings of classical economics therefore categorically rejected all such interventions. *Laissez faire et laissez passer!* Even Marxian socialists have not judged interventionism any differently from the classical liberals. They sought to demonstrate the absurdity of all interventionist proposals and labeled them contemptuously as "bourgeois." The ideology that is swaying the world today is recommending the very system of economic policy that is rejected equally by classical liberalism and older Marxism.

The problem of interventionism must not be confused with that of socialism. We are not dealing here with the question of whether or not socialism in any form is conceivable or realizable. We are not here seeking an answer to the question of whether human society can be built on public property in the means of production. The problem at hand is, What are the consequences of government and other interventions in the private property order? Can they achieve the result they are supposed to achieve?

A precise definition of the concept "intervention" is now in order.

1. Measures that are taken for the purpose of preserving and securing the private property order are not interventions in this sense. This is so self-evident that it should need no special emphasis. And yet it is not completely redundant, as our problem is often confused with the problem of anarchism. It is argued that if the state must protect the private property order, it follows that further government interventions should also be permissible. The anarchist who rejects any kind of state activity is said to be consistent. But he who correctly perceives the impracticability of anarchism and seeks a state organization with its apparatus of coercion in order to secure social cooperation is said to be inconsistent when he limits government to a narrow function.

Obviously, this reasoning completely misses the point. We are not here discussing the question of whether or not social cooperation can do without the organization of coercion, which is the state, or government. The sole point under discussion is whether there are only two conceivable possibilities of social organization with division of labor, that is, the public property order and the private property order—disregarding syndicalism—or whether there is yet a third system as assumed by interventionists, namely, a private property order that is regulated through government intervention. Incidentally, we must carefully distinguish between the question of whether or not government is necessary and the question of where and how government authority is in order. The fact that social life cannot do without the government apparatus of coercion cannot be used to conclude also that restraint of conscience, book censorship, and similar measures are desirable, or that certain economic measures are necessary, useful, or merely feasible.

Regulations for the preservation of competition do not at all belong to those measures preserving the private property order. It is a popular mistake to view competition between several producers of the same product as the substance of the ideal liberal economic order. In reality, the central notion of classical liberalism is private property, and not a certain misunderstood concept of free competition. It does not matter that there are many recording studios, but it does matter that the means of record production are owned privately rather than by government. This misunderstanding, together with an interpretation of freedom that is influenced by the natural rights philosophy, has led to attempts at preventing the development of large enterprises through laws against cartels and trusts. We need not here discuss the desirability of such a policy. But we should observe that nothing is less important for an understanding of the economic effects of a certain measure than its justification or rejection by some juristic theory.

2. Partial socialization of the means of production is not intervention in our sense. The concept of intervention assumes that private property is not abolished, but that it still exists in substance rather than merely in name. Nationalization of a railroad constitutes no intervention; but a decree that orders an enterprise to charge lower freight rates than it otherwise would is intervention.

3. Government measures that use market means, that is, seek to influence demand and supply through changes of market factors, are not included in this concept of intervention. If government buys milk in the market in order to sell it inexpensively to destitute mothers or even to

distribute it without charge, or if government subsidizes educational institutions, there is no intervention. (We shall return to the question of whether the method by which government acquires the means for such actions constitutes "intervention.") However, the imposition of price ceilings for milk signifies intervention.

Intervention is a limited order by a social authority forcing the owners of the means of production and entrepreneurs to employ their means in a different manner than they otherwise would. A "limited order" is an order that is no part of a socialist scheme of orders, that is, a scheme of orders regulating all of production and distribution, thus replacing private property in the means of production with public property.

J. Philip Wogaman (1948–) is a United Methodist minister in the Washington, D.C., area and author of *Economics and Ethics* (1986). Reverend Wogaman is critical of capitalism and free markets in general. In this selection he argues in favor of governmental intervention in the market as a matter of securing justice. His argument entails the market's lack of efficiency in justly distributing necessary goods and services.

◆ ◆ ◆

The case for allowing the free market to establish priorities is obviously persuasive to many people and, as we have said, it has enjoyed a resurgence in the past few years. Many more people, including even some socialists, believe that some use should be made of free-market institutions in the allocation of goods and services. But that would be as a part of a wider overall plan. Those who believe in real free-market allocation do not see this as part of a broader scheme; they see it as the place where the decisive priority-setting occurs. If they are right, then there is little point advising one another about the best stewardship of our personal resources. There would be no vantage point from which one could see the whole picture and no leverage point at which policy decisions could be reached to implement economic priorities for the entire community. So we are facing a watershed issue when we decide for or against reliance on the market mechanism to establish priorities for us.

During the first half of the twentieth century, most of Western capitalism countries decided they simply could not rely on this mechanism, at least not without combining it with a good deal of social planning. Practically speaking, too many people were being hurt economically in the process and too many public concerns were being neglected. In retrospect, one wonders how on earth President Reagan could ever have concluded that it hasn't "worked" to use the taxing power of government for purposes of social change. If anything hasn't *worked*, it would appear to be over reliance on the free market to do everything....

The outpouring of legislation in the Progressive and New Deal eras of twentieth-century America came in direct response to human need and social pressure. The exploitation of child labor (and of the labor of men and women), hazardous working conditions, dehumanizingly long hours of work, low wages, periodic times of depression with high unemployment, shoddy and dangerous products, ruin of the natural environment, racial, religious, and gender discrimination all evoked social exposé, popular outcry, and governmental intervention. Left alone, the free-market mechanism was increasing production all right, but it was devastating human society. It was widely perceived that some outside force had to intervene in the market to establish and protect social goals transcending sheer economic efficiency. It was as though society instinctively rebelled against the triumph of instrumental economic values over intrinsic social ones.

WAGES

Wages may be described as the price of labor. Clearly, the amount paid to workers is a cost incurred by the producer if he wishes to have an employment force. Wages are an exchange of labor for compensation. This relationship fits with the model of trading goods and services.

Wages can be seen as prices of products—in this case, the price of labor. Increased demand for a limited supply of high-skilled workers will result in increased wages for those workers. Additionally, wages for those workers will increase if their supply (available high-skilled workers) is reduced. Though wages are a cost of production in the accounting books, it is important to view them as the price of a service (labor), where the potential workers are the suppliers and the industries are the consumers.

A true free-market system would allow wages to be determined by the changes in the market and the free consent of workers and employers. However, many modern states have adopted a minimum wage, which acts as a price floor. The concept behind the minimum wage is that workers who need to support themselves and possibly a family must meet a certain living standard. The government sets a wage below which no employer may drop when paying employees. While this measure may benefit some entry-level employees with higher wages, the effects of a price floor create a surplus. In this case, it is a surplus of workers as employers' demand for workers drops when the price of labor is higher at the minimum wage. It has also been suggested that the increased wages brought about by minimum wage legislation also contribute to price inflation, thus creating a vicious cycle of increasing prices and wages.

Behind the principle of government-set wages are such concepts as the cost of living and the standard of living. Cost of living refers to the costs associated with basic needs, such as food, shelter, and clothing. Standard of living means that in a particular society, certain standards have been generally accepted as necessary for living at a dignified level.

In both instances, the government enacts laws to force employers to pay a minimum wage that would meet such levels of living.

With the advent of organized labor, wages for such workers have tended to rise in the twentieth century. Using collective bargaining and political clout, labor unions have been able to deal with employers on behalf of thousands of employees fighting for higher wages.

Many factors affect the price of labor (wages). These include government, labor unions, and attitudes of the employers and workers themselves. In most cases, the labor market fits the supply and demand model, which shows that the most efficient setting of wages is likely approximated by the natural tendencies of the labor market.

Gary Becker (1930–), a Nobel prize-winning Chicago economist, is best known for his work in the area of human capital. *Human capital* is a term that originated in economic literature and refers to the economic value, creativity, and productivity of the human person. Recently, Christian social thinkers have begun to adopt the term, supplementing the economic understanding of human capital with an understanding of the dignity of the human person. Consequently, human capital takes on a richer connotation in the sense of viewing people as created in the image and likeness of God with a calling to a creative, intelligent, and productive vocation. Becker's use of human capital underscores the idea that wages are really the price of labor. Furthermore, investment in education and other goods that build human capital will yield higher wages for many. The following selection was taken from Becker's, *Human Capital: A Theoretical and Empirical Analysis, with Special Reference to Education* (1980).

♦ ♦ ♦

Some activities primarily affect future well-being; the main impact of others is in the present. Some affect money income and others psychic income, that is, consumption. Sailing primarily affects consumption, on-the-job training primarily affects money income, and a college education could affect both. These effects may operate either through physical resources or through human resources. This study is concerned with activities that influence future monetary and psychic income by increasing the resources in people. These activities are called investments in human capital.

The many forms of such investments include schooling, on-the-job training, medical care, migration, and searching for information about prices and incomes. They differ in their effects on earnings and consumption, in the amounts typically invested, in the size of returns, and in the extent to which the connection between investment and return is perceived. But all these investments improve skills, knowledge, or health, and thereby raise money or psychic incomes....

... Passions are easily aroused on this subject and even people who are generally in favor of education, medical care, and the like often dislike the phrase "human capital" and still more any emphasis on its economic effects. They are often the people who launch the most bitter attacks on research on human capital, partly because they fear that emphasis on the "material" effects of human capital detracts from its "cultural" effects, which to them are more important.

Paul Heyne (1951–1999) was an economist at the University of Washington and the author of *The Economic Way of Thinking*. In the following selection, Heyne demonstrates how wage levels are subject to market forces. In other words, wages are really the price of labor and as such are determined by many of the same factors and rely on the subjective valuations of both the employer and the employee.

♦ ♦ ♦

It is probably true that prices and wages will be more likely to drift upward when the economy is close to "full" employment. The economic system always contains a great deal of internal movement: some industries grow, others decline, firms rise and fall, new production techniques are introduced, the composition of demand changes, people enter and leave the labor force. Resources must therefore be attracted continuously into particular employments through the offer of acceptable employment terms. But employers and employees do not have perfect information. They must search for what they want and incur the costs of that search.

In a period of low unemployment, the cost of finding a new job will, on average, be lower for employees than during a period of high unemployment. Employees will therefore be more ready to give up a job when they think the wage is unsatisfactory and begin searching for another. So employers will find it difficult to reduce wages.

Search costs for employers are higher in periods of low unemployment. And so employers will offer higher wages than they might otherwise be willing to offer in order to avoid making an extensive and costly search for the new employees they want and to reduce the risk of losing present employees, who would be expensive to replace.

The same argument applies to prices in product markets. When the company is operating close to capacity, it may be difficult to obtain additional supplies in a timely manner; and buyers may consequently be willing to offer higher prices rather than search for alternative sources of supply. In a period of high unemployment and substantial excess capacity, sellers will be shaving prices, because buyers are harder to find.

Pope Leo XIII from *Rerum Novarum* offers useful comments concerning the justice of wages. While economic principles determine wage levels in accord with market forces, Leo places as a primary social aim the notion of a just or living wage. The just wage is one that would allow a parent to support his or her family with a moderate quality of life. The Roman Catholic Church has always been clear that the normative principle of a just wage does not translate into actual price or wage levels. These actual numbers are determined by the market at the given time of analysis. The just or living wage is not intended to be imposed in defiance of market conditions, but rather is the goal to be achieved over time in light of productivity and cost reduction.

◆ ◆ ◆

Let it be granted then that worker and employer may enter freely into agreements and, in particular, concerning the amount of the wage; yet there is always underlying such agreements an element of natural justice, and one greater and more ancient than the free consent of contracting parties, namely, that the wage shall not be less than enough to support a worker who is thrifty and upright.

MONEY

Money is used as a medium of trade by its exchange for goods and service, or for alleviation of debt. The worth of goods and services may also be measured by equating their values in terms of money (or prices).

Money serves as a universal (within each system) commodity to be traded so that bartering for specific goods is not necessary. By using money to trade for a product, the task of finding a supplier who is interested in what you are willing to trade is eliminated; money is accepted in sale because it can be used as purchase power immediately.

Since money is a physical commodity with which to trade, it is necessary to explain how it holds value for those involved in the exchange. For economic purposes, there are three types of money. The first type deals directly with the value of the physical representation of money. The best example of this is a coin made of silver, gold, or other precious metal. The coin is traded and used as money because the coin itself actually has redeemable value for its precious metal. This type of money was most often used in medieval times, as trade occurred among different kingdoms.

A second type of money is that which has no physical, redeemable value, but is a kind of "promissory note" in that it represents such value. In other words, this money is backed by some object of wealth (usually a precious metal, like a bar of gold) and can be traded as if trading a piece of that object. The United States practiced the gold standard until the 1970s. Under this standard, the prices on bills and coins correlated to an amount of gold for which one could trade one's money.

The third type of money is commonly known as "fiat money." This is money that has no physical, redeemable value and has no object of wealth backing it. Usually the government sets a certain rate of value for the denominations of the money and declares that the money, by law, can be used for trade and the settlement of debts. The United States is currently on a system of fiat money, using paper bills and alloy coins for currency.

Monetary policy is important in systems of fiat money. If too much paper money is produced, the unit is devalued. Too much paper money in circulation can also lead to price inflation, while too little can deflate the economy. The Federal Reserve Board monitors the money-printing policies in the United States.

Money has evolved over time. In addition to coin currency and paper money, credit has further expanded the role of money. Checks and credit cards promise the payment of money later in exchange for a product now. Indeed, the use of credit has virtually become synonymous with money today.

With so many uses and its effect on the simplification of trade, it is no wonder that money is considered essential to modern economic systems.

Money is an often misunderstood economic phenomenon. Some Christians believe that money itself—and not necessarily the love of money—is the root of all evil. Others do not understand the origin or economic function of currency. In this selection from his *Politics*, **Aristotle (384–329 B.C.)** offers a clear explanation of both the origin and use of money. Naturally, the subject of money cannot be divorced from the concomitant topic of economic exchange. For what is money, if not a medium of exchange?

◆ ◆ ◆

All articles of property have two possible uses. Both of these uses belong to the article as such, but they do not belong to it in the same manner, or to the same extent. The one use is proper and peculiar to the article concerned; the other is not. We may take a shoe as an example. It can be used both for wearing and for exchange. Both of these uses are uses of the shoe as such.

Even the man who exchanges a shoe, in return for money or food, with a person who needs the article, is using the shoe as a shoe; but since the shoe has not been made for the purpose of being exchanged, the use which he is making of it is not its proper and peculiar use. The same is true of all other articles of property.

Exchange is possible in regard to them all: It arises from the natural facts of the case, and is due to some men having more, and others less, than suffices for their needs. We can thus see that retail trade [which buys from others to sell at a profit] is not naturally a part of the art of acquisition. If that were the case, it would only be necessary to practice exchange to the extent that sufficed for the needs of both parties [and not to the extent of the making of profit by one of the parties at the expense of the other].

In the first form of association, which is the household, it is obvious that there is no purpose to be served by the art of exchange. Such a purpose only emerged when the scope of association had already been extended [until it issued in the village]. The members of the household had shared all things in common: The members of the village, separated from one another [in a number of different households], had at their disposal a number of different things, which they had to exchange with one another, as need arose, by way of barter—much as many uncivilized tribes still do to this day....

[I]t was from exchange, as thus practiced, that the art of acquisition [in its second sense] developed, in the sort of way we might reasonably expect. [Distant transactions were the cause]. The supply of men's needs came to depend on more foreign sources, as men began to import for themselves what they lacked, and to export what they had in superabundance; and in this way the use of a money currency was inevitably instituted.

The reason for this institution of a currency was that all the naturally necessary commodities were not easily portable; and men therefore agreed, for the purpose of their exchanges, to give and receive some commodity [i.e., some form of more or less precious metal] which itself belonged to the category of useful things and possessed the advantage of being easily handled for the purpose of getting the necessities of life. Such commodities were iron, silver, and other similar metals.

Ludwig von Mises explains the role of money in a free economic system in this passage, which was taken from his classic work *Human Action.*

◆ ◆ ◆

The elementary theory of value and prices employs, apart from other imaginary constructions to be dealt with later ... the construction of a market in which all transactions are performed in direct exchange. There is no money; goods and services are directly bartered against other goods and services. This imaginary construction is necessary. One must disregard the intermediary role played by money in order to realize that what is ultimately exchanged is always economic goods of the first order against other such goods. Money is nothing but a medium of interpersonal exchange. But one must carefully guard oneself against the delusions which this construction of a market with direct exchange can easily engender.

The relation between the demand for money and the supply of money, which may be called the money relation, determines the height of purchasing power. Today's money relation, as it is shaped on the ground of yesterday's purchasing power, determines today's purchasing power. He who wants to increase his cash holding restricts his purchases and increases his sales and thus brings about a tendency toward falling prices. He who wants to reduce this cash holding increases his purchases—either for consumption or for production and investment—and restricts his sales; thus he brings about a tendency toward rising prices.

Changes in the supply of money must necessarily alter the disposition of vendible goods that are owned by various individuals and firms. The quantity of money available in the whole market system cannot increase or decrease otherwise than by first increasing or decreasing the cash holdings of certain individual members. We may, if we like, assume that every member gets a share of the additional money right at the moment of its inflow into the system, or shares in the reduction of the quantity of money. But whether we assume this or not, the final result of our demonstration will remain the same. This result will be that changes in the structure of prices brought about by changes in the supply of money available in the economic system never affect the prices of the various commodities and services to the same extent and at the same date.

Let us assume that the government issues an additional quantity of paper money. The government plans either to buy commodities and services or to prepay debts incurred or to pay interest on such debts. However, this may be, the treasury enters the market with an additional demand for goods and services; it is now in a position to buy more goods than it would buy before. The prices of the commodities it buys rise. If the government had expended in its purchases money collected by taxation, the taxpayers would have restricted their purchases and, while the prices of goods bought by the government would have risen, those of other goods would have dropped. But this fall in the prices of the goods the taxpayers used to buy does not occur if the government increases the quantity of money at its disposal without reducing the quantity of money in the hands of the public. The prices of some commodities— viz., of those the government buys—rise immediately, while those of the other commodities remain unaltered for the time being. But the process goes on. Those selling the commodities asked for by the government are now themselves in a position to buy more than they used previously. The prices of the things these people are buying in larger quantities therefore rise too. Thus the boom spreads from one group of commodities and services to other groups until all prices and wage rates have risen. The rise in prices is thus not synchronous for the various commodities and services.

When eventually, in the further course of the increase in the quantity of money, all prices have risen, the rise does not affect the various commodities and services to the same extent. For the process has affected the material position of various individuals to different degrees. While the process is under way, some people enjoy the benefit of higher prices for the goods or services they sell, while the prices of the things they buy have not yet risen or have not risen to the same extent. On the other hand, there are people who are in the unhappy situation of selling commodities and services when whole prices have not yet risen or not in the same degree as the prices of the goods they must buy for their daily consumption. For the former the progressive rise in prices is a boon, for the latter a calamity. Besides, when the debts come to an end, the wealth of various individuals has been effectively impoverished. Conditions are no longer what they were before. The mutual ratio of the money prices of the vendible goods and services is no longer the same as before. The price structure has changed apart from the fact that all prices in terms of money have risen. The final prices to the establishment of which the market tends after the effects of the increase in the quantity of money have been fully consummated are not equal to the previous final prices multiplied by the same multiplier.

MARGINAL UTILITY

Marginal utility is a term used to describe satisfaction gained by consumers when making trade decisions. It is derived from the notion of utility, which describes human behavior by asserting that people act and make decisions based on what they perceive as being the greatest benefit to themselves. In other words, people act to maximize their utility, where utility is the satisfaction or benefit people receive as a result of their decisions.

Marginal utility is an estimation of an individual's additional satisfaction from acquiring one more additional unit of the trade. For example, if a consumer is looking to purchase meat from a market, she considers several factors, such as prices of meats, quality, and location. When the consumer decides which pack of meat to buy, she subconsciously meets a level of utility. The consumer may wish to buy an additional pack of meat; she must consider what level of utility that extra pack will warrant. The difference between the utility of the second pack and the utility gained from the first pack is known as marginal utility.

Marginal utility is important in determining choices among traders. Since price is a restraining factor for consumers, price is usually compared with utility. Using the meat example again, if the marginal utility for purchasing a third pack of meat is still higher than the price, the consumer will most likely buy three packs of meat. As long as the marginal utility is higher than the price, more units should be obtained. What is known as the optimal amount is when the marginal utility for a certain number of units equals the price. For if marginal utility is lower than price, it is irrational to spend that extra money on something that will not give additional satisfaction equal to the amount of that money.

The concept of marginal utility often resembles a decreasing function at some point in the scale; that is, the more units attained, the smaller the marginal utility. In many cases, marginal utility can be traced as increasing to a certain point (the optimal point, where price equals marginal utility), at which time it will start to decrease. This means that obtaining more units is, in terms of marginal utility, better for consumers until they reach a number of units where marginal utility begins to decrease per unit. To use the meat example again, purchasing three packs may have high marginal utility because the consumer is assured of having enough to eat, to store, to give away, and so forth. But meat can spoil if it is not cooked within so many days, so buying six packs would have a lower marginal utility than price because of the chance the meat could go to waste.

Marginal utility is a concept that can be difficult to measure numerically. Usually numbers are assigned to help explain the process behind human decision making in economic systems. Using number values for marginal utility makes it easily comparable with price, an essential relationship among microeconomics.

Wilhelm Röpke (1899–1966), was a Lutheran economist primarily interested in the role of morality in the market. In this passage from *Economics of the Free Society* (1963), Röpke explains the concept of marginal utility and its central role in economic calculation. This selection not only explains the concept of marginal utility but also demonstrates other basic themes of free-market economics.

♦ ♦ ♦

[I]t is imperative that we keep clearly in mind that the economic system is not an objective mechanical thing which functions whether we will or no, but a process to which we all contribute in the totality of our reflections and our decisions. At bottom, it is the millions upon millions of subjective events taking place in the mind of each individual which form the substrata of economic phenomena. It is the feelings, judgments, hopes and fears of men which are manifested objectively in such things as prices, money, interest, prosperity and depression. But around what axis do these movements of the human psyche revolve? An answer to this question will provide us with the key to an understanding of all the objective events of economic life—to an understanding in brief, of the "phenomena of the market."

The meaning of all economic decisions and actions can be summed up in the word *economize*. When we have only a limited quantity of an important or useful commodity, we invariably tend to husband the inadequate supply. When we cannot have as much as we would like of a thing, there must be a certain order in our use of it if "waste" is to be avoided—if we wish, that is, to forestall our acting in an uneconomic manner....

Economic goods and not free goods determine our behavior. Our whole life is made up of decisions which seek to establish a satisfactory balance between our unlimited wants and the limited means at hand to satisfy them. To say that economic goods are limited in quantity is simply to say that the existing stocks of such goods are unable to satisfy the total subjective demand for them. It is important to note that this is not the same thing as objective scarcity....

When it comes to assigning a good its place on the scale of values, the determining factor is utility—not a general utility based on the degree of the good's vital importance, but the specific, concrete utility of a definite quantity of the good. The larger the supply of the good at our disposal, the smaller is the amount of satisfaction procured by its individual units, and hence the lower is such a good ranked on our scale of values. The reason for this is that with increasing satisfaction of a want, the utility (satisfaction or enjoyment) furnished by each successive dose diminishes. Moreover, take away any one of a number of identical units and the loss of utility or satisfaction will be the same as if any other had been taken away. It follows that the minimum utility of the one last dose or increment determines the utility of every other unit of the supply and therefore the utility of the whole supply. The value we attach to water is not determined by the infinite utility of the single glass of water needed to save us from perishing of thirst; it is determined by the utility of the last dose used to bathe ourselves or to sprinkle the flowers. We call the utility of this last dose *final* or *marginal utility*.

UNINTENDED CONSEQUENCES

In a system that does not practice pure free-market economics, government regulatory agencies are often active forces. When policies of regulation are enacted, the theory behind them does not predict the unintended consequences of the real world market.

Unintended consequences are any results in the market that are directly or indirectly caused by the regulation policies of government. Such consequences are unforeseen or not considered when the agency is putting together its course of action. By disrupting the natural flow of the economy, regulation policies designed for the betterment of society often create the byproducts of unintended consequences.

For example, much regulation occurs in public utility industries. These are industries that provide services to members of the public that are deemed to be necessary in society. Examples of such industries are telephone companies (local and long distance operators), electric companies, water providers, and the cable television industry. The government has decided that the public can best be served by allowing the industries to operate with limited competition but with heavy regulation. Though recent measures have been approved to begin deregulating some of these industries, the government's policies are still perpetuating the unintended consequences caused by regulation.

Unintended consequences can exist in many forms depending on the type of regulation being exercised. Regulation restricting trade often limits choices for consumers, as is the case with public utilities. With fewer choices, prices usually rise as well. Investment is also decreased, as potential investors know the rigid rules set by governmental agencies in the industries in which they may be interested lowers the possibility for profit. Innovation and development by the industries themselves are in many cases stemmed due to the regulation. These unintended consequences, resulting from policies aimed to aid society, ultimately cost the consumers, the industries themselves, and the economy as a whole.

In the United States, there is much regulation even in industries not labeled as public utilities. Food and drug manufacturers must adhere to standards set by the FDA, merging companies are monitored by the Department of Justice (DOJ) and FTC, and industrial firms are subject to rules made by the EPA and Occupational Safety and Hazard Administration (OSHA). The unintended consequences of limited trade and stringent regulations are felt by all involved. Even the government is hurt by such consequences, as stunted economic growth means fewer taxes for funding programs.

Though regulation may be enacted as a means of stabilizing economic systems, the unintended consequences that result serve as detriments to all involved in the trade process.

The selection below provides a helpful illustration of the law of unintended consequences; it was taken from **Henry Hazlitt's** *Economics in One Lesson.*

◆ ◆ ◆

Let us begin with the simplest illustration possible: Let us, emulating Bastiat, choose a broken pane of glass.

A young hoodlum, say, heaves a brick through the window of a baker's shop. The shopkeeper runs out furious, but the boy is gone. A crowd gathers, and begins to stare with quiet satisfaction at the gaping hole in the window and the shattered glass over the bread and pies. After a while the crowd feels the need for philosophic reflection. And several of its members are almost certain to remind each other or the baker that, after all, the misfortune has its bright side. It will make business for some glazier. As they begin to think of this they elaborate upon it. How much does a new plate glass window cost? Two hundred and fifty dollars? That will be quite a sum. After all, if windows were never broken, what would happen to the glass business? Then, of course, the thing is endless. The glazier will have $250 more to spend with other merchants, and these in turn will have $250 more to spend with still other merchants, and so ad infinitum. The smashed window will go on providing money and employment in ever-widening circles. The logical conclusion from all this would be, if the crowd drew it, that the little hoodlum who threw the brick, far from being a public menace, was a public benefactor.

Now let us take another look. The crowd is at least right in its first conclusion. This little act of vandalism will in the first instance mean more business for some glazier. The glazier will be no more unhappy to learn of the incident than an undertaker to learn of a death. But the shopkeeper will be out $250 that he was planning to spend for a new suit. Because he has had to replace a window, he will have to go without the suit (or some equivalent need or luxury). Instead of having a window and $250 he now has merely a window. Or, as he was planning to buy the suit that very afternoon, instead of having both a window and a suit he must be content with the window and no suit. If we think of him as a part of the community, the community has just lost a new suit that might otherwise have come into being, and is just that much poorer.

The glazier's gain of business, in short, is merely the tailor's loss of business. No new "employment" has been added. The people in the crowd were thinking only of two parties to the transaction, the baker and the glazier. They had forgotten the potential third involved, the tailor. They forgot him precisely because he will not now enter the scene. They will see the new window in the next day or two. They will never see the extra suit, precisely because it will never be made. They see only what is immediately visible to the eye.

James D. Gwartney (1955–) is professor of economics at Florida State University and currently serves as the chief economist for the joint economic committee of Congress. In his short but precise booklet, *What Everyone Needs to Know About Economics and Prosperity* (1993), he offers this insight about unintended consequences, what he calls *secondary effects*.

◆ ◆ ◆

Time and again, politicians stress the short-term benefits derived from a policy, while completely ignoring longer-term consequences. Similarly, there seems to be an endless pleading for proposals to help specific industries, regions, or groups without considering their impact on the broader community, including taxpayers and consumers. Of course, much of this is deliberate. When seeking political favors, interest groups and their hired representatives have an incentive to put the best spin on their case. Predictably, they will exaggerate the benefits, while ignoring important component costs. When the benefits are immediate and easily visible, while the costs are less visible and mostly in the future, it will be easier for interest groups to sell befuddled economic reasoning.

It is easy to point to instances where the secondary effects are largely ignored. Consider the case of rent controls imposed on apartments. Proponents argue that controls will reduce rents and make housing more affordable for the poor. Yes, but there are secondary effects. The lower rental prices will depress the rate of return on housing investments. Current owners of rental units may be forced to accept the lower return, but this will not be true for potential future owners. Many of them will channel their funds elsewhere; apartment house investments will fall; and the future availability of rental units will decline. Shortages will develop and the quantity of rental housing will fall with the passage of time. These secondary effects will not be immediately observable. Thus, rent controls command substantial popularity in communities ranging from New York City to Berkeley, California, even though a declining supply of rental housing, poor maintenance, and shortages are the inevitable results. In the words of Swedish economist Assar Lindbeck: "In many cases rent control appears to be the most efficient technique presently known to destroy a city—except for bombing."

PROFIT

Profit is the goal of economic actors and the ultimate incentive to firm operators in the free-market system. Profit is best described as total revenue minus the total costs of an individual business. If revenues exceed costs, the business is earning profit. If costs exceed revenues, the business is taking losses. And if revenues equal costs, the business is "breaking even."

When determining profit, it is important to understand all the costs that go into the equation. Keeping track of these costs is what often necessitates accounting departments for larger firms. Costs might include the price of materials, rent for a facility, wages paid to workers, marketing costs—anything that goes into the production of the firm's products. Accounting methods will separate costs into different categories, but when considering simple net profit, all costs are added together to be subtracted from total revenues for that period.

Revenues equal the price of the product multiplied by the quantity sold. Firms that diversify their product lines have different price-quantity combinations for different products. Additionally, as time progresses, price and quantity recommendations can change for the product (as can costs). Profit, then, can be measured in almost any period, such as days, weeks, months, and years.

When a company is earning profit, it retains the difference between total revenues and total costs. The incentive of profit in free-market systems is what drives firms to enter the market and compete with each other for consumers. More consumers partaking in a certain product line from one firm give it a profit advantage over another with similar costs. If the goal in the market is to obtain wealth, profit through trade is powerful motivation to provide what consumers demand at efficient costs to the company.

If a firm's costs exceed its revenues, it is carrying negative profit (loss). Such firms usually exit the market, as it is irrational to continue trading if it means losing money. If a fixed cost, such as rent for a building, is in effect until the end of a certain period (like a yearly lease), the firm may choose to continue operating while taking a loss as long as it can pay for such fixed costs. At the end of the period, the firm will then close its business. However, if the firm is taking such a loss that it cannot cover even its fixed costs, it will go out of business right away. Many such cases involve the firm filing for bankruptcy.

Some advocates of social orders have argued that pursuing profit is negative for society because companies will try to exploit consumers with higher prices and lower quality products (stemming from decreasing costs). Free-market thinkers believe the pursuit of profit benefits consumers because competition breeds lower prices, and consumers will naturally prefer high-quality products. Though the vagaries of both arguments are debatable, it is certain that profit provides incentive for businesses to succeed.

Wilhelm Röpke offers a positive view of the role of profit in this selection from *The Social Crisis of Our Time* (1942).

♦ ♦ ♦

A pure market system means that economic success can only be obtained by rendering an equivalent economic service to the consumer, and that at the same time, failure to do so is relentlessly punished by losses and finally by bankruptcy, which means expulsion from the ranks of those responsible for production (entrepreneurs). Income without equivalent performance and unpunished default (burdening someone else with the loss) are both prevented in this pure market system, which, as we shall show later, has been disastrously falsified by historical "capitalism." In order to achieve these ends, this economic system makes use of a double arrangement, first of all, the above mentioned system of competition and, secondly, the coupling of responsibility and risk (profit and loss chance). This coupling principle, according to which those who guide the productive process enjoy the profits of success and personally bear the full weight of failure, and those who take the chances of profit and loss guide productive processes, is one of the most important, even if increasingly adulterated principles of our economic system, and it would be difficult to prove that it is unnatural and does not fulfill its purpose.

At the same time we can now understand the true implications of the often criticized and morally condemned idea of profit, in which many people see nothing but a mask for anti-social self-seeking, greed, and unfair practices. But in reality the role of profit in the pure market economy consists in providing a reliable and irreplaceable yardstick for establishing whether an enterprise is going to be a successful part of the national economic structure or not. Under the rule of profit the entrepreneur who adapts himself, receives from the market an acknowledgement to that effect in the form of a bonus, but the entrepreneur who does not fit in is penalized by the market. As a rule the reward is as high as the penalty is harsh, but it is precisely this that leads to an especially effective selection of the managers of the productive process. Since the fear of loss is probably always greater than the striving for gain, we may say that in the last resort our economic system is regulated by fear of bankruptcy. The socialist state would have to create an equivalent for all this: In the place of profit it would have to put another yardstick of success and another system of selection of the managers of production, in the place of bankruptcy it would have to put another penalty for failure. It is, however, very doubtful whether such an equivalent can be found. Up to now, at any rate, it has not been discovered.

Alfred Marshall (1842–1924), an English economist, defined economics as the study of the material rewards for work. In elaborating on this definition, he particularly sought to emphasize the productive aspects of market activity. The following selection was taken from Marshall's *Principles of Economics* (1890).

♦ ♦ ♦

Economics is a study of men as they live and move and think in the ordinary business of life. But it concerns itself chiefly with those motives which affect, most powerfully and most steadily, man's conduct in the business part of his life. Everyone who is worth anything carries his higher nature with him into business; and, there as elsewhere, he is influenced by his personal affections, by his conceptions of duty and his reverence for high ideals. And it is true that the best energies of the ablest inventors and organizers of improved methods and appliances are stimulated by a noble emulation more than by any love of wealth for its own sake. But, for all that, the steadiest motive to ordinary business work is the desire for the pay which is the material reward of work. The pay may be on its way to be spent selfishly or unselfishly, for noble or base ends; and here the variety of human nature comes into play. But the motive is supplied by a definite amount of money: and it is this definite and exact money measurement of the steadiest motives in business life, which has enabled economics far to outrun every other branch of the study of man....

Basil the Great (330–379), a Cappadocian monk, earned the title "the Great" because of his superb reputation as an ecclesiastical statesman, reformer of liturgy, and social activist. More than any other patristic writer, Basil emphasizes the social purpose of riches, the limitations and the social function of the right to private ownership, and the duty of sharing one's possessions. The following excerpts were taken from his homily titled "I Will Pull Down My Barns." In these selections, Basil sharply criticizes the rich for their lack of social consciousness and insists upon sharing as an essential obligation of social justice. In other words, profit, while morally legitimate, requires the virtues of generosity and magnanimity.

♦ ♦ ♦

The wealth you handle belongs to others; think of it accordingly. Not for long will it delight you; soon it will slip from you and be gone, and you will be asked to give strict account of it. Yet you keep it all locked away behind doors and sealed up; and then the thought of it keeps you awake at nights; you take counsel about it inwardly, and your counsellor is yourself—a fool. "What can I do?" How easy it would have been to say: "I will fill the souls of the hungry; I will open my barns; I will invite all the poor. I will be like Joseph in his charitable summons; I will speak generous words—All you who have need of loaves, come to me; each shall have his fill from God's bounty, which flows for all." But that is not your way; no; you grudge men satisfaction; you contrive evil schemes within your soul; you are not concerned how to distribute to each according to his needs but how to get everything yourself and keep everyone from using it.

Imitate the earth; bring forth fruit as it does; shall your human status be inferior to a lifeless thing? The earth brings forth fruits not for its own pleasure but for your service; you can reap for yourself the fruit of all generosity because the rewards of good works return to those who offer them. If you give to the hungry, the gift becomes your own and comes back to you with increase. As the wheat falling on the ground turns to gain for the man who lets it fall, so the grain bestowed on the hungry brings you profit a hundredfold hereafter. Make the end of husbandry the beginning of heavenly sowing. "Sow for yourselves unto justice," the Scripture says (Hos. 10:12). Why then be anxious, why torture yourself, why strive to shut in your riches with bricks and mortar? "A good name is better than great riches" (Prov. 22:1). And if you admire riches for the honor they bring, consider which is more glorious—to be called the father of children innumerable, or to have gold pieces innumerable in your purse. Your money you must leave behind you, whether you will or not, but the glory of good works you will bear with you to the Master, when a whole people, standing about you before their judge and yours, call you their foster-father and benefactor and all the names won by charity....

SUPPLY AND DEMAND

Supply and demand are concepts that act as the backbone of economic study. Since economics studies trade between those offering a commodity and those desiring to obtain such a commodity, studying the supply of and demand for that commodity is essential.

Supply is the side of the dichotomy that refers to the tendencies of those providing goods or services to be traded in the market. In microeconomics, the supply function represents a single firm's trends, while macroeconomics utilizes a notion of supply that aggregates the supply in all existing firms from one industry. The concept of supply illustrates firms' attitudes when producing goods for sale on the market.

Representing consumer attitudes is the demand side of the relationship. Demand describes the consumers' attitudes toward certain products available in the market. Microeconomic demand represents a particular group's demand for a good, while macroeconomics leans toward the study of aggregate demand over time. By comparing supply and demand, analyses of the actions of consumers and producers can be made and predictions ventured.

In order to illustrate the relationship between supply and demand, it is common to represent them on a graph. Along the x-axis, figures are measured in quantity; the y-axis is measured in price. This type of graph displays the natures of supply and demand functions as they relate to the price and quantity of the good in question.

To represent supply tendencies, a "supply curve" is drawn on the graph. It is widely accepted that supply curves in the free-market model act in a positive manner, that is, as x increases, so does y increase, and vice versa. The supply curve is shown to originate at a given point and will then rise upward and from left to right at varying rates. The reason for this tendency in the supply curve is that as prices for products increase (the y figure), producers will want to increase the quantity at which these goods are sold. So, price and quantity increase together in the supply curve (though they can increase at different rates).

The demand curve behaves in a different way. Most agree that demand curves, according to free-market economics, generally adhere to a negative relationship, or that as *x* or *y* is increasing, the other is decreasing (sometimes at different rates). The demand curve then appears to be sloping downward, left to right, upon beginning at a certain point on the graph. The demand curve slopes downward because, as prices of the good increase, they are inclined to purchase smaller quantities of that product. On the other hand, as prices fall, consumers will be more willing to buy greater quantities of the good. So, according to the demand curve, price and quantity will be opposite each other in terms of increasing or decreasing figures.

When placed on the same graph, the supply and demand curves can model many trends in free-market economics. Where the supply and demand curves intersect, an *x* and a *y* figure may be obtained. The *x* value stands for the optimal quantity at which the supplier produces and the consumers demand the good. The value of *y* represents the optimal price for both the producer to charge and the consumer to pay for the good. Of course, this model is for the free-market system, but the consumers and producers do not have to behave in this manner. Higher prices can be charged or smaller quantities produced, but the relationship in these ways can predict shortages, surpluses, changes in attitudes, et cetera by using the graph as a tool for study.

Only the mere basics of the supply and demand relationship have entered this discussion. These are fundamental to economic study but the relationship can become far more complex when other supply and demand models are considered.

Frank Knight explains the basics of supply and demand in this excerpt from *The Economic Organization* (1951).

◆ ◆ ◆

It is a trite saying that "price is determined by demand and supply." Like many other facts which "everyone knows," this is true or false according to the interpretation, and unfortunately the correct interpretation is not an easy task. In order to explain price and the way in which price functions as a regulating force in economic life, it has to be understood in several different interpretations. The main difficulty is that, as often happens, causal relationships run in one direction from one point of view and in the other direction from another.... In the case of these terms, demand and supply, there is obviously a sense in which price determines both, while in a different sense it is being determined by them. A satisfactory explanation of price requires drawing several rather careful distinctions between different uses of these words. In particular, it is necessary to distinguish different meanings according to whether immediate or ultimate relations are to be considered, whether price is to be explained from a short-run or a long-run point of view.

The actual price at any given moment of a standard commodity like wheat, whose price is constantly determined by free competitive dealing in an open market, is fixed by speculative traders who typically are neither producers, nor, to any significant extent, consumers of the commodity. They are literally, "middlemen." Neither producers nor consumers have anything to say about the price. The demand and supply which fix what we shall designate as the actual or momentary or speculative price are the buying and selling activities of traders. Yet it is clear that the buying and selling of traders is in a larger view determined by the amounts which the real consumers will buy and which the producers will sell. So that the price which is immediately determined by speculators' demand and supply is finally determined by consumers' demand and producers' supply. But still another distinction is necessary. For the producers cannot change their supply until a minimum period of time has passed—in the case of wheat, a year or more. The supply for any one year is practically fixed at the amount which has been produced. In a longer time, however, producers can change the amount produced, and will do so, according to conditions which affect the profits in their business. From this third point of view, the demand is the consumers' demand and the supply the producers' supply, as before, but over a period of years the supply is under control, whereas with reference to a single year it is not. Again, the supply will be very different according to whether the conditions of production and sale are those of competition or of monopoly. We must attempt to state the different principles and the relations between them, briefly yet with considerable care to be accurate, as there is no other way to avoid confusion. The notion of a market first calls for a few words.

Paul Heyne lays out the basic principles of supply and demand analysis in this passage from *The Economic Way of Thinking.*

♦ ♦ ♦

Supply and demand analysis is the most basic tool in the economist's kit. To master the economic way of thinking, you must learn to think in terms of supply and demand. The beginning step is to convince yourself that all the important factors affecting exchange can usually be divided into two categories: factors affecting demand and factors affecting supply. Step two is to become comfortable in the company of demand curves and supply curves....

What will happen to the price of wheat and to the amount harvested in the United States if the wheat crop fails disastrously in Russia and Ukraine? The first question to ask is whether that crop failure will affect the demand or the supply in the United States. Because U.S.-grown wheat is an excellent substitute for wheat grown elsewhere, a large crop failure elsewhere will increase the demand for U.S. wheat.... That will cause the price to rise because the quantity demanded at the old price will now be greater than the quantity supplied.... This higher price will in turn cause a larger quantity of wheat to be supplied.

Which will increase more? The price or the quantity supplied? That is going to depend on the elasticity of supply. If a small price increase leads to a large percentage increase in the quantity supplied, the supply is elastic. In that case, a large increase in demand will raise the price of wheat just a little while substantially increasing the quantity of wheat available for sale. On the other hand, if even a very large percentage increase in the price produces just a small increase in the amount offered for sale, the supply is inelastic, and a large increase in demand will result in a much higher price but little increase in the amount of wheat made available for purchase.

DIVISION OF LABOR

The division of labor is a concept that originated around the time of the Industrial Revolution and ultimately contributed to the rise of the free-market system. It is the principle of the separation of tasks within a system of creating products, where each task is a specialized activity within the overall process.

Division of labor enables goods to be produced one after another in succession. Before the method was utilized, goods had to be produced by either one person or a few people who worked on every aspect of the production. The principle of the division of labor enables one to concentrate on only one aspect of production. By focusing on one facet of the good an employee is able to work on more products in the same period of time. To illustrate, think of assembling a car. If a worker's responsibility is to install the car's wheels, he could accomplish this many more times in one day than if he had to build the entire car himself.

Each worker must have a specialized task within the process with the goal of completing the final product. Placing wheels on a car would be pointless if no one installed an engine, brakes, or steering column. The advantage of dividing up labor is being able to produce many more products in the same time one could produce a few with employees working on every aspect of production.

The idea of the division of labor gained primacy with the support of Henry Ford in the early 1900s. To manufacture his automobiles, Ford incorporated the concept of the division of labor into the assembly line. The autos would move throughout the factory, and at each station would receive different production attention. This method allowed Ford to produce automobiles at an unheard-of rate, and the assembly line is still used today.

The division of labor often required more workers for the system to function smoothly. Some may wonder why this is not a negative, as wages paid to workers clearly are production costs. As explained above, however, more products can be manufactured in less time, and the producer thus collects more revenue. The costs of hiring more workers to operate the division of labor is usually offset or exceeded by the revenues received because of the large quantities of products placed on the market.

In an even larger sense, the division of labor is applied across the market. Farmers grow vegetables, processors package them, truckers transport them, and supermarkets sell them to the public. Four different industries are involved in getting vegetables to the market for consumers. Thus, the division of labor functions beyond the mere production of goods.

Participation in free-market economics usually implies seeking the goal of attaining profit. With the division of labor, revenues are increased while production costs are justified. Division of labor, then, is an important aspect of free-market systems.

Adam Smith provided perhaps the first systematic exposition of the division of labor and its beneficial economic consequences. What follows is the core of his argument, extracted from *The Wealth of Nations*.

◆ ◆ ◆

This division of labour, from which so many advantages are derived, is not originally the effect of any human wisdom, which foresees and intends that general opulence to which it gives occasion. It is necessary, though very slow and gradual consequence of a certain propensity in human nature which has in view no such extensive utility; the propensity to truck, barter, and exchange one thing for another.

Whether this propensity be one of those original principles in human nature, of which no further account can be given; or whether, as seems more probable, it be the necessary consequence of the faculties of reason and speech, it belongs not to our present subject to enquire. It is common to all men, and to be found in no other race of animals, which seem to know neither this nor any other species of contacts.... In almost every other race of animals each individual, when it is grown up to maturity, is entirely independent, and in its natural state has occasion for the assistance of no other living creature. But man has almost constant occasion for the help of his brethren, and it is in vain for him to expect it from their benevolence only. He will be more likely to prevail if he can interest their self-love in his favour, and shew them that it is for their own advantage to do for him what he requires of them. Whoever offers to another a bargain of any kind, proposes to do this. Give me that which I want, and you shall have this which you want, is the meaning of every such offer; and it is in this manner that we obtain from one another the far greater part of those good offices which we stand in need of. It is not from the benevolence of the butcher, the brewer, or the baker, that we expect our dinner, but from their regard to their own interest. We address ourselves, not to their humanity but to their self-love, and never talk to them of our own necessities but of their advantages. Nobody but a beggar chooses to depend chiefly on the benevolence of his fellow-citizens. Even a beggar does not depend on it entirely. The charity of well-disposed people, indeed, supplies him with the whole fund of his subsistence. But though this principle ultimately provides him with all the necessaries of life which he has occasion for, it neither does nor can provide him with them as he has occasion for them. The greater part of his occasional wants are supplied in the same manner as those of other people, by treaty, by barter, and by purchase. With the money which one man gives him he purchases food. The old cloaths which another bestows upon him he exchanges for other old cloaths which suit him better, or for lodging, or for food, or for money, with which can buy either food, cloaths, or lodging, as he has occasion.

Frederic Bastiat emphasizes the positive, cooperative aspects of the division of labor in this excerpt from an essay "What is Seen and What is Not Seen."

◆ ◆ ◆

If society were not a very real association, anyone who wanted a suit of clothes would be reduced to working in isolation, that is, to performing himself the innumerable operations in this series, from the first blow of the pickaxe that initiates it right down to the last thrust of the needle that terminates it.

But thanks to that readiness to associate, which is the distinctive characteristic of our species, these operations have been distributed among a multitude of workers, and they keep subdividing themselves more and more for the common good to the point where, as consumption increases, a single specialized operation can support a new industry. Then comes the distribution of the proceeds, according to the portion of value each one has contributed to the total work. If this is not association, I should like to know what is.

Note that, since not one of the workers has produced the smallest particle of raw material from nothing, they are confined to rendering each other mutual services, to aiding each other for a common end; and that all can be considered, each group in relation to the others, as *middlemen*. If, for example, in the course of the operation, transportation becomes important enough to employ one person; spinning, a second; weaving, a third; why should the first one be considered more of a *parasite* than the others? Is there no need for transportation? Does not someone devote time and trouble to the task? Does he not spare his associates this time and trouble? Are they doing more than he, or just something different? Are they not all equally subject, in regard to their pay, that is, their share of the proceeds, to the law that restricts it to the *price agreed upon after bargaining*? Does not this division of labor and these arrangements, decided upon in full liberty, give the common good? Do we, then, need a socialist, under the pretext of planning, to come and despotically destroy our voluntary arrangements, put an end to the division of labor, substitute isolated efforts for cooperative efforts, and reverse the progress of civilization?

Is association as I describe it here any the less association because everyone enters and leaves it voluntarily, chooses his place in it, judges and bargains for himself, under his own responsibility, and brings to it the force and the assurance of his own self-interest? For association to serve the name, does a so-called reformer have to come and impose his formula and his will on us and concentrate within himself, so to speak, all of mankind?

TAXES

Taxes are fees collected by governments from their citizenry in order to pay for official programs and government projects. Paying taxes is most often mandatory and enforced by national law. Governments set the rates at which taxes are paid and in the manner they are paid.

In the United States, the Internal Revenue Service (IRS) administers tax collection, and revenues are accounted for once a year. The government's revenue through taxation is placed in the general treasury fund monitored by the Department of the Treasury. Then, usually through legislation, Congress determines how the taxes will be spent in various government programs.

Taxes can come in many forms. The United States currently has several taxable goods or events, some of which include the income tax, the sales tax, the capital gains tax, and the inheritance tax. State and local governing bodies may also have their forms of these or other taxes. Tax credits also exist for those earning negative revenues (loss) in certain areas. The government will pay back taxes or waive the payments of portions of other taxes when tax credits are applied.

The income tax is a certain amount removed from one's paycheck during employment. Today, the employer is obligated to withhold a certain amount of your pay, which goes directly to the government. The rate of income tax is set by legislation; the rate of tax one pays usually increases as one's income does. Income tax includes taxes levied on paychecks, as well as on interest earned on money in savings.

The sales tax is an extra amount charged to products purchased. These tax rates are usually set by state governments, and can range anywhere from two to nine percent (meaning that for every dollar paid, an additional $.02–$.09 must be paid in taxes). Vendors are responsible for charging customers and then transferring to government the revenues collected in sales tax. There is a special type of sales tax known as the luxury tax.

Luxury taxes are sales taxes, usually much higher than traditional sales tax rates, applied only to certain items deemed possibly enjoyable but unnecessary by the government. The tax on cigarettes is a common example of the luxury tax.

A capital gains tax is the fee charged when revenues are made from investments. Any profits made by trading in the securities exchange are subject to tax. Conversely, however, any loss suffered in the market will usually allow for a tax credit.

There also exits the category of the inheritance/estate/gift tax. These are taxes assessed when gifts are made from one to another. Taxes are assessed when inheritance is accepted, an estate makes a payment, or a gift of some value is given from one person to another.

The level of taxes set by the government usually depends on the types of political and economic systems that are in place. A free-market society would have very low tax rates and few categories of tax. Tax revenue would pay for sustaining public goods, such as a national defense system and a law enforcement/justice system. A more socialist (statist) government, on the other hand, would have much higher tax rates and more taxable events. They would use this revenue to offer government-provided services, such as health care, transportation, and development.

Taxation is a major issue today in the mixed economy of the United States. Choosing how to balance government revenues with individual earnings is a debate that is expected to last as long as elected officials with differing opinions are making policy decisions.

Once again we turn to **Adam Smith**, this time for a classic exposition on the nature of taxation and its negative effects on the economy. This selection is taken from *The Wealth of Nations*.

◆ ◆ ◆

The private revenue of individuals, it has been shown in the first book of this inquiry, arises ultimately from three different sources; Rent, Profit, and Wages.... Every tax must finally be paid from some one or other of those three different sorts of revenue, or from all of them indifferently. I shall endeavour to give the best account I can, first, of those taxes which, it is intended, should fall upon rent; secondly, of those which, it is intended, should fall upon profit; thirdly, of those which, it is intended, should fall upon wages; and, fourthly, of those which, it is intended, should fall indifferently upon all those three different sources of private revenue. The particular consideration of each of these four different sorts of taxes will divide the second part of the present chapter into four articles, three of which will require several other subdivisions. Many of those taxes, it will appear from the following review, are not finally paid from the fund, or source of revenue, upon which it was intended they should fall.

Before I enter upon the examination of particular taxes, it is necessary to premise the four following maxims with regard to taxes in general.

I. The subjects of every state ought to contribute towards the support of the government, as nearly as possible, in proportion to their respective abilities; that is, in proportion to the revenue which they respectively enjoy under the protection of the state. The expense of government to the individuals of a great nation, is like the expense of management to the joint tenants of a great estate, who are all obliged to contribute in proportion to their respective interests in the estate. In the observation or neglect of this maxim consists, what is called the equality or inequality of taxation. Every tax, it must be observed once and for all, which falls finally upon one only of the three sorts of revenue above-mentioned, is necessarily unequal, in so far as it does not affect the other two. In the following examination of different taxes I shall seldom take much further notice of this sort of inequality, but shall, in most cases, confine my observations to that inequality which is occasioned by a particular tax falling unequally even upon that particular sort of private revenue which is affected by it.

II. The tax which each individual is bound to pay ought to be certain and not arbitrary. The time of payment, the manner of payment, the quantity to be paid, ought all to be clear and plain to the contributor, and to every other person. Where it is otherwise, every person subject to the tax is put more or less in the power of the tax-gatherer, who can either aggravate the tax upon any obnoxious contributor, or extort, by the terror of such aggravation, some present or perquisite to himself. The uncertainty of taxation encourages the insolence and favours the corruption of an order of men who are naturally unpopular, even where they are neither insolent nor corrupt. The certainty of what each individual ought to pay is, in taxation, a matter of so great importance, that a very considerable degree of inequality, it appears, I believe, from the experience of all nations, is not near so great an evil as a very small degree of uncertainty.

III. Every tax ought to be levied at the time, or in the manner in which it is most likely to be convenient for the contributor to pay it. A tax upon the rent of land or of houses, payable at the same term at which such rents are usually paid, is levied at the time when it is most likely to be convenient for the contributor to pay; or, when he is most likely to have wherewithal to pay. Taxes upon such consumable goods as are articles of luxury, are all finally paid by the consumer, and generally in a manner that is very convenient for him. He pays them by little and little, as he has occasion to buy the goods. As he is at liberty, too, either to buy, or not to buy as he pleases, it must be his own fault if he ever suffers any inconsiderable inconveniency from such taxes.

IV. Every tax ought to be contrived as both to take out and to keep out of the pockets of the people as little as possible, over and above what it brings into the public treasury of the state. A tax may either take out or keep out of the pockets of the people a great deal more than it brings into the public treasury, in the four following ways. First, the levying of it may require a great number of officers, whose salaries may eat up the greater part of the produce of the tax, and whose perquisites may impose another additional tax upon the people. Secondly, applying to certain branches of business which might give maintenance and employment to great multitudes. While it obliges the people to pay, it may thus diminish, or perhaps destroy some of the funds, which might enable them more easily to do so. Thirdly, by the forfeitures and other penalties which those unfortunate individuals incur who attempt unsuccessfully to evade the tax, it may frequently ruin them, and thereby put an end to the benefit which the community might have received from the employment of their capitals. An injudicious tax offers a great temptation to smuggling.... But the penalties of smuggling must rise in proportion to the temptation. The law, contrary to all ordinary principles of justice, first creates the temptation, and then punishes those who yield to it; and it commonly enhances the punishment too in proportion to the very circumstance which ought certainly to alleviate it, the temptation to commit the crime.... Fourthly, by subjecting the people to the frequent visits, and the odious examination of the tax-gatherers, it may expose them to much unnecessary trouble, vexation, and oppression; and though vexation is not, strictly speaking, expense, it is certainly equivalent to the expense at which every man would be willing to redeem himself from it. It is in some one or other of these four different ways that taxes are frequently so much more burdensome to the people than they are beneficial to the sovereign.

Bibliography in Selected Readings

Definition of Economics

Hazlitt, Henry. *Economics in One Lesson.* New York: Crown Trade Paperbacks, 1979.

Knight, Frank H. *Risk, Uncertainty, and Profit.* New York: Sentry Press, 1964.

Mises, Ludwig von. *Human Action.* San Francisco: Fox & Wilkes, 1966.

Property

Bastiat, Frederic. *The Law.* Irvington-on-Hudson: Foundation for Economic Education, 1996.

Menger, Carl. *Principles of Economics.* Grove City, Penn.: Libertarian Press, 1994.

Leo XIII. Encyclical Letter *Rerum Novarum* (May 15, 1891).

Saint Augustine of Hippo. "Possessions Become Good Through the Goodness of Their Possessors." In *Social Thought.* Vol. 20. Edited by Peter C. Phan. Wilmington, Del.: Michael Glazer, 1984.

Saint John Chrysostom. "On the Social Function of Property," "On the Duty of the Rich." In *Social Thought.* Vol. 20. Edited by Peter C. Phan. Wilmington, Del.: Michael Glazer, 1984.

Saint Thomas Aquinas. *Summa Theologiae.* Harrison, N.Y.: Roman Catholic Books, 1992.

Smith, Adam. *The Wealth of Nations.* New York: E. P. Dutton & Co., 1938.

Trade

Keynes, John Maynard. *The General Theory of Employment, Interest, and Money.* New York: Harcourt, Brace, and Company, 1936.

Marx, Karl. "The Fetishism of Commodities." In *Essential Works of Socialism.* Edited by Irving Howe. Chicago: Holt, Rinehart, & Winston, 1970.

Mises, Ludwig von. *Socialism.* Indianapolis: Liberty Classics, 1981.

Saravia de la Calle, Luis. "On Entrepreneurial Activity and Trading." In *Instrucción de Mercaderes.* Madrid, 1949.

MUTUALLY BENEFICIAL EXCHANGE

Gilder, George. *Recapturing the Spirit of Enterprise.* San Francisco: ICS Press, 1992.

Novak, Michael. *The Catholic Ethic and the Spirit of Capitalism.* New York: Free Press, 1993.

Opitz, Edmund A. *Religion and Capitalism: Allies, Not Enemies.* New Rochelle, N.Y.: Arlington House, 1970.

VALUE AND PRICE THEORIES

De Lugo, Juan. *De Iustitia et Iure.* Lyon, 1642.

Keynes, John Maynard. *The General Theory of Employment, Interest, and Money.* New York: Harcourt, Brace, and Company, 1936.

Kirzner, Israel M. *Perception, Opportunity and Profit: Studies in the Theory of Entrepreneurship.* Chicago: University of Chicago Press, 1979.

Marx, Karl. *Capital: A Critique of Political Economy.* 4th ed. Edited by Friedrich Engels. New York: Modern Library, 1906.

Menger, Carl. *Principles of Economics.* Grove City, Penn.: Libertarian Press, 1994.

Molina, Luis de. *La Teoria del Justo Prico.* Madrid: Ed. Nacional, 1981.

Ricardo, David. "On the Principles of Political Economy and Taxation." In *The Works and Correspondence of David Ricardo.* Edited by Piero Sraffa. Cambridge: University Press for the Royal Economic Society, 1953.

Schumacher, E. F. *Small Is Beautiful.* New York: Harper and Row, 1955.

Taylor, Thomas C. *An Introduction to Austrian Economics.* Auburn, Ala.: The Ludwig von Mises Institute, 1988.

INTERVENTION

Friedman, Milton and Rose. *Free to Choose.* New York: Avon, 1979.

Mises, Ludwig von. *A Critique of Interventionism.* New Rochelle, N.Y.: Arlington House Publishers, 1976.

National Council of Catholic Bishops. *Economic Justice for All.* Washington, D.C.: National Conference of Catholic Bishops, 1986.

Wogaman, J. Philip. *Economics and Ethics.* Philadelphia: Fortress Press, 1986.

WAGES

Becker, Gary S. *Human Capital.* Chicago: University of Chicago Press, 1993.

Heyne, Paul. *The Economic Way of Thinking.* Englewood, N.J.: Prentice Hall, 1997.

Leo XIII. Encyclical Letter *Rerum Novarum* (May 15, 1891).

MONEY

Aristotle. *Politics.* New York: Oxford University Press, 1958.
Mises, Ludwig von. *Human Action.* San Francisco: Fox & Wilkes, 1966.

MARGINAL UTILITY

Röpke, Wilhelm. *Economics of the Free Society.* Chicago: Henry Regnery Company, 1963.

UNINTENDED CONSEQUENCES

Gwartney, James D. and Richard L. Stroup. *What Everyone Needs to Know About Economics and Prosperity.* Tallahassee, Fla.: James Madison Institute, 1993.
Hazlitt, Henry. *Economics in One Lesson.* New York: Crown Trade Paperbacks, 1979.

PROFIT

Basil the Great. Homily on "I Will Pull Down My Barns." In *Social Thought.* Vol. 20. Edited by Peter C. Phan. Wilmington, Del.: Michael Glazer, 1984.
Marshall, Alfred. *Principles of Economics.* 9th ed. Vol. 1. Edited by C. W. Guillebaud. New York: Macmillan, 1961.
Röpke, Wilhelm. *The Social Crisis of Our Time.* New Brunswick, N.J.: Transaction Publishers, 1992.

SUPPLY AND DEMAND

Heyne, Paul. *The Economic Way of Thinking.* Englewood, N.J.: Prentice Hall, 1997.
Knight, Frank H. *The Economic Organization.* New York: Harper and Row, 1951.

DIVISION OF LABOR

Bastiat, Frederic. "What Is Seen and What Is Not Seen." In *Selected Essays on Political Economy.* Toronto: D. Van Nostrand, 1964.
Smith, Adam. *The Wealth of Nations.* New York: E. P. Dutton & Co., 1938.

TAXES

Smith, Adam. *The Wealth of Nations.* New York: E. P. Dutton & Co., 1938.

ABOUT THE AUTHOR

Samuel Gregg is a moral philosopher who has written and spoken extensively on ethics in public policy, business ethics, as well as Catholic social teaching. He has an M.A. in political philosophy from the University of Melbourne, and a Doctor of Philosophy degree in moral philosophy from the University of Oxford, which he attended as a Commonwealth Scholar. He is the author of several books, monographs, and articles that study questions ranging from moral philosophy to issues of corporate governance. In 2000, he was awarded the Friedrich von Hayek Fellowship by the Mont Pèlerin Society and was elected as a Fellow of the Royal Historical Society in 2001. He is presently director of the Center for Economic Personalism at the Acton Institute in Grand Rapids, Michigan, a member of the Faculty of the John Paul II Pontifical Institute (Melbourne Campus) within the Pontifical Lateran University, and an adjunct scholar at the Centre for Independent Studies in Sydney, Australia.

Suggested Reading List

Christian Social Thought

Beisner, E. Calvin. *Prosperity and Poverty.* Wheaton, Ill.: Crossway Books, 1988.

Boff, Leonardo and Clodovis. *Salvation and Liberation.* Maryknoll, N.Y.: Orbis Books, 1987.

Buttiglione, Rocco. *Karol Wojtyla: The Thought of the Man Who Became Pope John Paul II.* Grand Rapids, Mich.: Eerdmans Publishing Company, 1997.

Catechism of the Catholic Church. Mahwah, N.J.: Paulist Press, 1994.

Cronin, John F. *Catholic Social Principles.* Milwaukee: Bruce Publishing Company, 1950.

Gay, Craig M. *With Liberty and Justice for Whom? The Recent Evangelical Debate Over Capitalism.* Grand Rapids, Mich.: Eerdmans Publishing Company, 1991.

Grasso, Kenneth L., Gerard V. Bradley, and Robert P. Hunt, eds. *Catholicism, Liberalism, and Communitarianism: The Catholic Intellectual Tradition and the Moral Foundations of Democracy.* Lanham, Md.: Rowman and Littlefield, 1995.

Gregg, Samuel. *Challenging the Modern World: Karol Wojtyla/John Paul II and the Development of Catholic Social Teaching.* Lanham, Md.: Lexington Books, 1999.

Gutierrez, Gustavo. *A Theology of Liberation.* Maryknoll, N.Y.: Orbis Books, 1973.

Henry, Carl F. *Aspects of Christian Social Ethics.* Grand Rapids, Mich.: Eerdmans Publishing Company, 1964.

John XXIII. Encyclical Letter *Mater et Magistra* ("Christianity and Social Progress," 1961). Boston: Daughters of St. Paul.

John Paul II. Encyclical Letter *Centesimus Annus* ("On 100 years," 1991). Boston: Daughters of St. Paul.

_____. Encyclical Letter *Sollicitudo Rei Socialis* ("On Social Concern," 1987). Boston: Daughters of St. Paul.

_____. Encyclical Letter *Laborem Exercens* ("On Human Work," 1981). Boston: Daughters of St. Paul.

Kuyper, Abraham. *Lectures on Calvinism.* Grand Rapids, Mich.: Eerdmans Publishing Company, 1994.

Leo XIII. Encyclical Letter *Rerum Novarum* ("On the Condition of the Working Classes," 1891). Boston: Daughters of St. Paul.

Marshall, Paul. *Thine Is the Kingdom: A Biblical Perspective on the Nature of Government and Politics Today.* Grand Rapids, Mich.: Eerdmans Publishing Company, 1984.

Messner, Johannes. *Social Ethics: Natural Law in the Modern World.* St. Louis: B. Herder, 1965.

Murray, John Courtney, S.J. *We Hold These Truths: Catholic Reflections on the American Proposition.* New York: Sheed and Ward, 1960.

Nash, Ronald H. *Social Justice and the Christian Church.* Milford, Mich.: Mott Media, 1983.

National Conference of Catholic Bishops. *Economic Justice for All.* Washington, D.C.: Confraternity of Christian Doctrine, 1986.

Neuhaus, Richard John. *Doing Well and Doing Good: The Challenge to the Christian Capitalist.* New York: Doubleday, 1992.

O'Brien, David J. and Thomas A. Shannon, eds. *Renewing the Earth: Catholic Documents on Peace, Justice, and Liberation.* Garden City, N.J.: Image Books, 1977.

Olasky, Marvin. *The Tragedy of American Compassion.* Washington, D.C.: Regnery, 1992.

Paul VI. Encyclical Letter *Populorum Progressio* ("On the Development of Peoples," 1967). Boston: Daughters of St. Paul.

Pius XI. Encyclical Letter *Quadragesimo Anno* ("On Social Reconstruction," 1931). Boston: Daughters of St. Paul.

Van Til, Henry R. *The Calvinistic Concept of Culture.* Grand Rapids, Mich.: Baker Book House, 1959.

Weigel, George, ed. *A New Worldly Order: John Paul II and Human Freedom.* Lanham, Md.: Ethics and Public Policy Center, 1992.

_____. *Soul of the World.* Grand Rapids, Mich.: Eerdmans Publishing Company, 1996.

Wogaman, J. Philip. *Economics and Ethics.* Philadelphia: Fortress Press, 1986.

CHRISTIANITY AND ECONOMICS

Novak, Michael. *Business As a Calling.* New York: Free Press, 1996.

_____. *The Catholic Ethic and the Spirit of Capitalism.* New York: Free Press, 1993.

_____. *The Spirit of Democratic Capitalism.* Lanham, Md: Madison Books, 1991.

Opitz, Edmund A. *Religion and Capitalism: Allies, Not Enemies.* New Rochelle, N.Y.: Arlington House, 1970.

Rasmussen, D. and D. Den Uyl. *Liberty and Nature*. La Salle, Ill.: Open Court Publishing, 1991.

Sirico, Robert A. *Economics, Faith and Moral Responsibility*. New Zealand: The Center for Independent Studies, 1993.

Tice, D. J. "Conservatism Versus Consumerism." *The St. Croix Review* 30 (June 1997): 6–11.

Weigel, George and Robert Royal, eds. *Building the Free Society*. Grand Rapids, Mich.: Eerdmans Publishing Company, 1993.

ECONOMICS

Bastiat, Frederic. *The Law*. Irvington-on-Hudson, N.Y.: Foundation for Economic Education, 1996.

Becker, Gary. *Human Capital: A Theoretical and Empirical Analysis, with Special Reference to Education*. 2d ed. Chicago: University of Chicago Press, 1983.

Friedman, Milton and Rose. *Free to Choose*. New York: Avon, 1979.

Galbraith, John Kenneth. *The Affluent Society*. Boston: Riverside Press, 1958.

Gilder, George. *Recapturing the Spirit of Enterprise*. San Francisco: ICS Press, 1992.

____. *Wealth and Poverty*. San Francisco: ICS Press, 1993.

Gwartney, James and Richard Stroup. *What Everyone Should Know About Economics and Prosperity*. Tallahassee, Fla.: James Madison Institute, 1993.

Hayek, Friedrich A. *The Constitution of Liberty*. Chicago: University of Chicago Press, 1960.

____. *The Road to Serfdom*. London: George Routledge & Sons, 1944.

Hazlitt, Henry. *Economics in One Lesson*. New York: Crown Trade Paperbacks, 1979.

Heyne, Paul. *The Economic Way of Thinking*. Englewood, N.J.: Prentice Hall, 1997.

Keynes, John Maynard. *The General Theory of Employment Interest and Money*. New York: Harcourt, Brace, and Company, 1936.

Kirzner, Israel M. *Perception, Opportunity, and Profit*. Chicago: University of Chicago Press, 1979.

____. *The Meaning of Market Process*. New York: Routledge, 1992.

Knight, Frank H. *Risk, Uncertainty, and Profit*. New York: Sentry Press, 1964.

____. *The Economic Organization*. New York: Harper and Row, 1951.

Marshall, Alfred. *Principles of Economics*. 9th ed. Vol. 1. Edited by C. W. Guillebaud. New York: Macmillan, 1961.

Marx, Karl. *Capital: A Critique of Political Economy*. 4th ed. Edited by Friedrich Engels. New York: Modern Library, 1906.

Menger, Carl. *Investigations into the Methods of the Social Sciences*. New York: New York University Press, 1985.

____. *Principles of Economics*. Grove City, Penn.: Libertarian Press, 1994.

Mises, Ludwig von. *A Critique of Interventionism.* New Rochelle, New York: Arlington House, 1976.

_____. *Human Action: A Treatise on Economics.* 3d ed., rev. Chicago: Contemporary Books, 1966.

_____. *Socialism.* Indianapolis: Liberty Classics, 1981.

_____. *The Ultimate Foundation of Economic Science.* Kansas City: Sheed, Andrews, and McMeel, 1962.

Ricardo, David. *The Principles of Political Economy and Taxation.* Homewood, Ill.: R. D. Irwin, 1963.

_____. *The Works and Correspondence of David Ricardo.* Edited by Piero Sraffa. Cambridge: University Press for the Royal Economic Society, 1953.

Röpke, Wilhelm. *Economics of the Free Society.* Chicago: Regnery, 1963.

_____. *Civitas Humana.* London: Hodge, 1948.

_____. "Robbing Peter to Pay Paul: On the Nature of the Welfare State." In *Against the Tide.* Chicago: Regnery, 1969.

Rothbard, Murray. *Man, Economy, and State: A Treatise on Economic Principles.* Auburn, Ala.: Ludwig von Mises Institute, 1993.

Saravia de la Calle, Luis. "On Entrepreneurial Activity and Trading." In *Instrucción de Mercaderes.* Madrid, 1949.

Schumacher, E. F. *Small Is Beautiful.* New York: Harper and Row, 1918.

Smith, Adam. *An Inquiry into the Nature and Causes of the Wealth of Nations.* New York: E. P. Dutton & Co., 1938.

Taylor, Thomas C. *An Introduction to Austrian Economics.* Auburn, Ala.: Ludwig von Mises Institute, 1988.

Vaughn, Karen I. *Austrian Economics in America.* Cambridge: Cambridge University Press, 1994.

SOCIAL THEORY

Aristotle. *The Politics of Aristotle.* Edited and translated by Ernest Barker. New York: Oxford University Press, 1958.

Aquinas, Thomas. *Summa Theologiae.* Harrison, N.Y.: Roman Catholic Books, 1992.

Budziszewski, J. *Written on the Heart: The Case for Natural Law.* Downers Grove, Ill.: InterVarsity Press, 1997.

Calvin, John. *Institutes of the Christian Religion.* Edited by John T. McNeill. Translated by Ford Lewis Battles. Philadelphia: Westminster, 1960.

Finnis, John. *Natural Law and Natural Right.* Oxford: Clarendon Press, 1980.

Howe, Irving, ed. *Essential Works of Socialism.* Chicago: Holt, Rinehart, & Winston, 1970.

Mounier, Emmanuel. *Personalism.* Notre Dame: University of Notre Dame Press, 1952.

Röpke, Wilhelm. *The Social Crisis of Our Time.* New Brunswick, N.J.: Transaction Publishers, 1992.

Sandoz, Ellis, ed. *Political Sermons of the American Founding Era.* Indianapolis: Liberty Press, 1991.

Smith, Barry. *Austrian Philosophy.* Chicago: Open Court, 1994.